Real Bloomsbury

Also in the Real Wales series
Editor: Peter Finch

Real Aberystwyth – Niall Griffiths
Real Cardiff – Peter Finch
Real Cardiff Two – Peter Finch
Real Cardiff Three – Peter Finch
Real Liverpool – Niall Griffiths
Real Llanelli – Jon Gower
Real Merthyr – Mario Basini
Real Newport – Ann Drysdale
Real Swansea – Nigel Jenkins
Real Wales – Peter Finch
Real Wrexham – Grahame Davies

Real Bloomsbury

nicholas murray

series editor: peter finch

SEREN

Seren is the book imprint of
Poetry Wales Press Ltd
Nolton Street, Bridgend, Wales
www.serenbooks.com

Reprinted 2013

ISBN 978-1-85411-526-3

A CIP record for this title is available from the British Library

The publisher works with the financial assistance of the Welsh Books Council

Printed by Berforts Information Press, Stevenage

CONTENTS

WEST

SERIES EDITOR'S INTRODUCTION

I come at Bloomsbury up what was once bohemian Goodge Street, past Quartet Books and the newly painted Fitzrovia pub, to spill out among replacement sewer diggers, snarled up traffic and tourist hoards onto Tottenham Court Road. Home of electronics – Sony, Pioneer, Denham, Kenwood, Phillips – always was – from Xbox to handhelds, motherboards to modems, Walkmen to the unlocked imported desirable cell phone. Tottenham Court Road, the district's western boundary, this land of squares and green park, upmarket slice of the borough of Camden, place of space and Georgian style, university and medicine, literature and fame.

Bloomsbury is delineated by Euston, King's Cross and the international transit lounge that is St Pancras to the north; the ragged end of Oxford Street, the British Museum, Bloomsbury Way and Theobalds Road to the south; and the line of Grays Inn Road to the east. How will I know when I have arrived? By the change of pace now Soho and the panic of Oxford Street are behind me. By the green trees and the birds in the air. By the sense of English literature's still vibrant past that permeates the peaceful squares and ancient houses.

This is a district, nonetheless, that was barely here at the time of the great London fire. What became Bloomsbury Square had been laid out by the landowner, The Earl of Southampton, but not built. His plaza (originally known as Southampton Square) set the standard and the style for many of London's railinged but open spaces which followed.

What I am expecting is a place full of traffic with style wiped from its surface by twenty-first century greed and bustle. What I get is totally different. This is London's literary epicentre, after all. Dickens lived here, his house is now a museum. What became known as the Bloomsbury Group – those markers of twentieth century modernism clustering around Virginia Woolf – resided in Gordon Square, Anthony Trollope was born on Keppel Street, Gertrude Stein spent a winter living on Bloomsbury Square, George Orwell used the University of London Senate House on Malet Street as the inspiration for the Ministry of Truth in *Nineteen Eighty-Four*. T.S. Eliot worked at Faber and Faber on Russell Square. Yeats lived in north Bloomsbury for almost twenty-five years.

I'm eating the best and least expensive scrambled-egg on toast in

London, made by an Italian and served with speed, at a table mid Woburn Walk. I look up and there's the plaque on the wall above the restaurant. William Butler Yeats Irish Poet And Dramatist Lived In This House From 1895 To 1919. I'm in the university quarter now. Bloomsbury houses as much academic education as it does creative literature and, for that matter, medicine. The University of London campus fills the space between the gloriously domed British Museum and the architecturally reluctant Euston.

Everywhere there are plazas, piazzas, squares. Spaces of light and leaf, unsullied by trashed wheelie bin and sink estate gouged grass. Bedford Square. Russell Square. Brunswick Square. Gordon Square. Tavistock Square. Mahatma Ghandi's statue sits under the trees of this latter place. Fellow peace campaigners and conscientious objectors are memorialised nearby. On the wall of the BMA is a plaque commemorating the thirteen victims of the Tavistock Square bus bombing of 2005. Their names are as international as the United Nations.

There are hotels in abundance. From the Royal National Hotel on Bedford Way, London's largest, sleeping more than 3000 on a full night and the sort of brutalist concrete creation that's every hotel user's nightmare, to the stream of Georgian boutiques that line Gower Street. In succession I passed eight of them: Ridgemont Hotel, Arosfa Hotel, Arran Hotel, Hotel Cavendish, Regency Hotel, Garth Hotel, Jesmond Hotel, and the Gower Hotel. The run was only broken by the intervention of the Institute of Measurement and Control. No one would ever dream of sleeping there.

Some of Bloomsbury's gentle crescents retain their Bath-like sense of slow turning space. Cartwright Gardens, for example, remains faced by trees in full foliage slothfulness. In Georgian North Crescent, however, they've filled the space with an art deco monstrosity that was formerly a deep-level shelter and D-Day communications centre, linked to the Cabinet War Rooms by pneumatic dispatch tube. The Eisenhower Centre (or the Ei enhover Centre looked after by Recall, Total Information Management, as the sign is today) would be demolished if it were elsewhere. As things are the Crescent and the Centre co-exist in mutual hatred. There's a war memorial surrounded by railings built into the Eisenhower's car park. Or maybe that was originally the other way around. Nothing is completely perfect, including Bloomsbury.

I discover more bookshops than in a digital age I might have expected. A specialist in Arabic books in Burton Street. Skoob Books at the Brunswick Centre, squashed between Waitrose, the Territorial Army and Hunter Street Health Centre. A great tumble at Judd's second-hand bookshop on Marchmont Street. The Judd Street Gang were notorious nineteenth century Bloomsbury hooligans. High Stakes racing bookshop on Great Ormond Street. Gays the Word on Marchmont Street opposite a blue plaque marking the residence of comic actor Kenneth Williams. More in the University area.

There's a Bloomsbury face-off here between student land with its posters and graffiti and the calm cool style that Georgian money left behind. The more I walk the more it seems that money has won.

In the east the child becomes increasingly evident. Not just physically – although the independent Coram's Fields built on the site of the city's first foundling hospital mark out Bloomsbury's predilection. Adults may only enter if accompanied by a child reads the sign on the gate. Great Ormond Street runs east west housing the most famous children's hospital in the world. Near Brunswick Square stands the Foundling Museum, restored Georgian, telling the tale of Thomas Coram's hospital for unwanted eighteenth century London children and closed when I get there. It's Monday.

It's also possible to cross Bloomsbury in a doctor's white coat and not look in the least out of place. The Eastman Dental Hospital is on Gray's Inn Road. In Bloomsbury too are the Royal National Throat, Nose and Ear Hospital, The University College Hospital, and the National Hospital for Neurology and Neurosurgery. Mix those with an unexpectedly high evidence of trade union headquarters and a sense of schizophrenia begins to rise. Both Unite and Unison have offices here. Just along from the Rocket on Euston Road there's a giant billboard demanding that we fight the Tory cuts. With what, I wonder.

South of the great stations, in an area that could have taken the street dross moved on from King's Cross when St Pancras International was developed, stands St Pancras Parish Church. This is the new one, built in 1822 by W. and H.W. Inwood and based on the Ionic Temple of the Erectheum on the Acropolis in Athens. The church is huge, columned, and has an octagonal tower of the winds high above it. Christianity has left a thunderous mark. This one still active, engaging itself with the local community whenever and wherever it can. The crypt, filled with the coffined bones of nineteenth century worthies has been largely cleared and is in use as a gallery when I arrive. Paintings hanging on niche walls, dark passages over cold stone floors leading from one neo-gothic painting to the next. Scenes of gashed velvet, faded blood, lace dresses frail with age, black and white photographs of gay men and ungay women splashed by water. While I am there a photographer snaps a disrobed coupled lying across the slabs. There is more than a hint of the impermanence of the past. The show will be gone by the time you read this. But Bloomsbury's capacity to invent and inflame will no doubt continue.

Balancing the true splendour of Christianity's Ionic columns in the north are those of the British Museum in the south. Here international humanity in its surging number flow through Britain's centre for the artefacts of history. This is western influenced history in the main, and since it is that which has changed the way the whole world works then why should the museum not present it. The mummies of Egypt, the vases of the Greeks, the Rosetta Stone, the Elgin Marbles, the Cyrus Cylinder, the Sutton Hoo treasure, the Benin bronzes and half a dozen other world objects claimed by others. There is enough life-changing human reality in this place to keep the visitor onsite for weeks. Norman Foster's redevelopment of the central court literally dazzles. It is a place where humanity's achievements overwhelm us by their sheer number.

I retreat, exhausted, to the snub end of Oxford Street, the fringe of Bloomsbury, not in the district at all Nicholas Murray would say. Here, at Café Nero, it's still possible to sit in a leather chair and drink a Frappé Latte priced at less than three pounds and to do this without hearing any English spoken for at least 20 minutes. Refreshed I return for a second attack, this time with the text of Nicholas Murray's *Real Bloomsbury* in hand. How much did I miss in my first sweep? A considerable amount, it seems. Bloomsbury, district of layers and space and style and light. More fame per square metre than anywhere else in London. Nicholas Murray, excavator, reporter, author, foreigner, resident. The perfect alternative handbook maker. *Real Bloomsbury*, how the place actually is.

Peter Finch

PREFACE

Even in the heart of a great world city the spirit of neighbourhood prevails. Vast as London, Paris, New York, Madrid, Athens are in their metropolitan sprawl, the inhabitants live their lives day by day in one or other distinctive *quartier*. We wake, emerge to buy a newspaper, a pint of milk, or board a bus in a familiar locality, not inside some great abstraction known as 'the capital'. Attachment to the idea of place is universal and many of inner London's communities feel a sense of rootedness in their patch that is every bit as strong as that felt in a rural village. Bloomsbury is no exception. Tidal waves of tourists and students wash over this network of streets and squares. It has a vast floating, temporary population, but the locals still greet each other, relishing the human scale of small, intimate daily encounters, liking the feel of their patch, its quirks and quiddities.

This book is written by someone who has lived in the heart of Bloomsbury for more than a dozen years, splitting my life between it and my home in the Welsh Marches. It is a frankly personal essay but one based on real daily observation, combined with detailed historical and literary research.

But how does one write the profile of a city, of a distinctive space within the city? In my head are countless examples of city-writing I admire – Edmund White on Paris, John Banville on Prague, any number of authors on Venice or Oxford or Athens. The inimitable Peter Ackroyd on London's biography. I have even written my own book about my native city, Liverpool, and I know the pitfalls of trying to satisfy all of the urbanites all of the time. There is Gillian Tindall's wonderful onion-peeling of one area of north London (just north of our patch) *The Fields Beneath*, and her more recent *Footprints in Paris*, Jacques Réda's *Les Ruines de Paris*, Alex Karme's search for more than just the history of one building in *A Corner in the Marais*, Léon-Paul Fargue's *Le Piéton de Paris*, Georges Perec's *Tentative d'épuisement d'un lieu parisien*, that brilliant and inimitable intense observation of one tiny spot in Paris across several days. Why so many Parisian examples? Perhaps because the French are the consummate *flâneurs*, relishers of the urban space, café-dwellers, and people-watchers, whose capital city is often more hospitable to the relaxed, exploratory wanderer than crowded, hurrying, brusque, even rude, contemporary London. And Bloomsbury is now the transit lounge between London and Paris, the first place the Eurostar traveller hits when emerging from St Pancras International.

And then, in the world of fiction, there is Joyce's Dublin, Kafka's Prague, Paul Auster's New York...

In the end, I sit down and write what I see and think and feel. Think of this book as a stroll around an area that can be covered (and has been many times in the writing of it) entirely on foot: I hope you enjoy the walk.

* * *

WHAT IS BLOOMSBURY?

I think of the thousands who daily arrive at London's St Pancras International, from Paris or Vienna – or less exotically from Market Harborough or Luton – and of their emergence from the railway station into the ugly roar of traffic in Euston Road. I hear them ask: is this it? Is this the glamorous world capital I thought I was arriving at? Will it ever be possible to get over this road with the most pedestrian-unfriendly controlled crossings in London? What a honking, siren-screaming, scruffy, unappetising bit of cityscape I seem to have fetched up in. Arrival at the Gare du Nord, one might reflect, shabby as in some sense it is, nonetheless lets you know instantly that you are in Paris. There are welcoming bars and brasseries. It looks as it should.

Surely this is going to get better.

The opportunity eventually comes. My imaginary arrival crosses successfully, reaching the opposite pavement like someone disembarking with relief on a friendly shore after a rough crossing by boat. Their feet have touched Bloomsbury, the *flâneur*'s natural habitat. They will have no further need of public transport. Everything in this famous quarter of central London can be covered easily on foot. There are a couple of Underground stations but they won't be needing them.

Bloomsbury. Why is this word so resonant? The answer,

as plenty of those blue plaques indicating where famous people resided show, is the Bloomsbury Group, that early twentieth century constellation of literary talent with which the British have a lively love-hate relationship. On the one hand we profess to loathe their 'snobbery' (they were almost without exception socially superior and could be haughty in their fluting put-downs of people whom they considered not quite out of the right drawer, though generally professing an enlightened and progressive politics) whilst at the same time we are also forced to admit that Virginia Woolf, Lytton Strachey, Vanessa Bell, John Maynard Keynes, Katherine Mansfield, Bertrand Russell, and younger temporary acolytes like Aldous Huxley, were amongst the most talented writers, thinkers, artists of their epoch. And as for the snobbery, why is it that endless gossipy accounts of 'the Bloomsberries' sell when we ostensibly pretend that we don't want to hear any more about them? I will be coming back to the Bloomsbury Group later, because they are unignorable and left their mark on Bloomsbury for all time, but for now it's worth making the basic point that the combination of their name and the very high density of university buildings, research institutions, teaching hospitals, museums, libraries and galleries in the area means that the word 'Bloomsbury' will always vibrate with a literary-intellectual resonance whenever it is pronounced.

But Bloomsbury has many other faces, which this book will explore.

From the time of the early manor of Bloomsbury, with its fields and duck ponds and hayricks, a rural phase that lasted well into the eighteenth century when its development as a district of elegant aristocratic houses and garden squares began, Bloomsbury has always been a rather special part of central London.

It has had its fashionable and unfashionable times such as the late nineteenth and early twentieth century – when Henry James could turn up his nose at "dirty Bloomsbury"[1], V.S. Pritchett refer to the "spiritless streets of Bloomsbury"[2] and Ford Madox Ford evoke his

"Bloomsbury of dismal, decorous, unhappy, glamorous squares".[3] In this shabby late Victorian and Edwardian epoch the music hall jokes started about "Bloomsbury landladies" who mothered actors and poets and other doubtful categories of tenant in multi-occupied and shabby Georgian houses. But Bloomsbury has continued to stand, solid and spacious, and maybe just a little staid and institutional in parts. In spite of the presence of all those literary Bohemians and young people packed into student halls of residence, it can lack a certain lightness and vivacity, strike some people as heavy and ponderous, in spite of the light and space granted by the great garden squares.

Pritchett said: "I still think that the London mind has more back than front to it."[4] He meant that Londoners take pride in their city's past and are sentimental and nostalgic about its traditions. This is not Manhattan and it certainly isn't Brasilia. London has never been neophiliac. The past thrusts itself at you with every step you take, especially if you are on foot, peering down odd cobbled alleyways and deserted mews, looking up at old inscriptions and eighteenth century fanlights over imposing doors. Ford Madox Ford, however, felt this was a danger, believing that a writer on the city must set out to record the here and now, using only so much history as was needed to ballast the present. The author's job was to "make the Past, the sense of all the dead Londons that have gone to the producing of this child of all the ages, like a constant ground-bass beneath the higher notes of the Present" – otherwise you get "a very false and a very sentimental rendering of London."[5]

Point taken.

WHERE IS BLOOMSBURY?

There is no precise, administrative political boundary marking off Bloomsbury. The Bloomsbury electoral ward of the London Borough of Camden (where I live) covers quite a limited segment of central Bloomsbury and, for the purposes of this book, I have drawn four big bold black lines around the district I am going to explore. The line to the north is Euston Road. In the south, the marker is Theobalds Road running westward into Bloomsbury Way and then New Oxford Street. The slightly wonky rectangle is completed by Gray's Inn Road in the east and Tottenham Court Road to the west (let's not mess with the Fitzrovia boys). This is a pegging out of the territory that is coherent, hangs together and feels more or less right, even if the raunchy north east fringes near King's Cross, for example, give off a different reek from the cosy squares around the University where Lytton and Virginia romped.

And now, with all due respect to Ford Madox Ford, it's time for just a little bit of history. And etymology.

I do my thinking about Bloomsbury on my feet, as a dedicated city walker, but sometimes I manage to sit down, and today I find myself in Tavistock Square, not far from that Euston Road tumult I have just described, on an empty park bench. In this Square, Virginia Woolf one morning got the idea for *To The Lighthouse* and Dickens wrote both *Hard Times* and *Little Dorrit* and started *Bleak House*. My hypothetical Eurostar arrival will be starting to get the idea about Bloomsbury, but for me what the name suggests is not the obvious literary-intellectual ambience, the universities and institutions, the museums and squares. It's the sense of *space*. So many areas of inner London are crowded and dense with people and cars – gentrified terraced streets with tiny front gardens concreted over to provide parking for yet another gas-guzzler – that the amount of open space in Bloomsbury, the garden squares, the huge extent of Coram's Fields, Russell Square – the largest square in London if you don't count Lincoln's Inn Fields – can't fail to strike you. A Parisian might think that an odd thing to say. There are no grand boulevards or vast paved squares, but I am talking about a crowded little island, and comparing it with other parts of London. Until the eighteenth century this was open fields, frequented by courting couples, brawling youths, duellists, and occasional fairground showmen and promoters of wrestling-booths. I'm not saying it's like my Radnorshire village (where we humans are outnumbered by sheep) but it's unusually well-endowed with public open space. And the memory, the psychic trace, of those open fields is something I think I can still feel here.

Before Bloomsbury became an inhabited place, there was the City of London, penned behind its walls and gates even after the Romans had left – though the medieval Londoners superimposed a crooked and quirky Anglo-Saxon street pattern on the rigid Roman grid. Inevitably, the urban mud began to ooze out of the City but it was a slow process. Elizabethan edicts tried to reduce the spread of new building but (a constant theme in Bloomsbury history) the pull was always to the fashionable West, towards Westminster and the court. All along the Thames in the Strand the wealthy bishops in their big houses or 'inns' scorned the northern bucolic wilderness running towards the heights of Highgate and Hampstead. Gradually houses started to appear along Holborn, the main thoroughfare from the City to the West End, but they too faced firmly south, with their backs to the farmland. It was still to be a long time before speculative housing started to creep northwards.

WHY BLOOMSBURY?

Although I am more sympathetic than many to the Bloomsbury group's concrete achievements, I am as capable as the next person of being irritated by a certain kind of Bloomsbury Group anecdote, full of condescending Stracheyan *hauteur*, and on these occasions I console myself with the thought that 'Bloomsbury' shared its etymological origins with a stinking open sewer. William Blemund, the first known owner of the Blemundsbury estate ('bury' meaning a manor house, the area originally part of the 'berwick' or sub-division of the manor of Totenhale or Tottenham) is first mentioned around 1160 as witness to various deeds. The twelfth century historian, William Fitzstephen, has a pleasant description of the Arcadian landscape of London, including Bloomsbury, around 1180:

> On the north Side are the Pastures and plain Meadows, with Brooks running through them, turning Water-mills, with a pleasant noise. Not far off is a great Forest, a well-wooded Chace, having good Covert for Harts, Bucks, Does, Boars, and wild Bulls. The Corn Fields are not of a hungry sandy mould, but as the fruitful Fields of Asia, yielding plentiful Increase and filling the Barns with Corn. There are, near London, on the north Side, especial Wells in the Suburbs, sweet, wholesome, and clear. Amongst which, *Holywell, Clarkenwell* and *St. Clement's-well,* are most famous, and most frequented by Scholars and Youths of the City, in Summer Evenings, when they walk forth to take the Air.[6]

Blemund's son, also William, later constructed or canalised a watercourse known as Blemund's Ditch, which is mentioned in thirteenth century documents and sometimes called Bloomsbury Great Ditch or Southampton Sewer. By the nineteenth century it was known as a "common sewer", but it then became part of that submerged network of watercourses – like the famous Fleet river which skirts my patch to the east – that lies under the London streets.

When they built the Imperial Hotel in Russell Square in 1902 it was reported that an ancient stream had been uncovered which might have had some connection to the Bloomsbury Ditch.[7] The Ditch actually formed the southern boundary of the Bloomsbury Manor, separating it from the adjacent Manor of St Giles.

In the thirteenth century the Bloomsbury Estate was confiscated after William de Kent, the husband of Blemund's niece, Egidia, was imprisoned in Windsor Castle in the winter of 1265 for opposing Henry III at the battle of Evesham in the civil war. Then the trail gets muddy and confused until a wealthy fishmonger and Member of Parliament, Nicholas Exton, pops up to acquire the Estate in 1369. In a nimble bit of property management, Nick the fishmonger promptly handed it over to Edward III who then passed it on to the new Carthusian monastery known as London Charterhouse, with an arrangement that Exton and his wife would receive £40 a year as long as they lived. But at the Dissolution of the Monasteries, around 1538, all the Charterhouse land, including the Manor of Bloomsbury, was seized by Henry VIII.

Some of the old London histories and guidebooks pursued more fanciful etymologies. William Maitland, for example, in his *The History of London from its Foundation to the Present Time* (1769), claimed the derivation was from Lomsbury but doesn't say who or what 'Lom' might have been.

The real turning point for Bloomsbury came in 1545 when Henry VIII granted the estate or 'messuage' of 'Blumsburye', the fields running northwards, and 'Fygge meadowes', to his Lord Chancellor, Thomas Wriothesley, who was made the first Earl of Southampton two years later in 1547. Half the estate consisted of the so-called Hundred Acres of arable land, pasture and meadow. Two of the Earl's farming tenants, John Butler and John Hyde, delivered him five cartloads of hay annually in lieu of their thirty-bob rent. The Dukes of Bedford, who are Wriothesley's descendants, still own much of Bloomsbury in the twenty-first century, administering it through the

Bedford Estates. This is a story whose thread I will take up later.

And I will be back in Tavistock Square.

NORTH

EUSTON ROAD: WOULD YOU ADAM AND EVE IT?

I am standing at the far north-western corner of Bloomsbury, at the top of Tottenham Court Road where it meets Euston Road, in front of the shiny new Accident and Emergency department of University College Hospital. I turn my back on Warren Street Underground Station (opened in 1907 as part of the original Charing Cross, Euston and Hampstead Railway and initially known as Euston Road station) which stands to the west like the circular bastion of a small fortress defending the territory of Fitzrovia. Outside the A&E, whose vast reception desk can be seen through the plate glass windows, there is a constant coming and going of distressed people, waiting to hear what has happened to their friends and relatives, sending their reports by phone, talking excitedly into them, sending urgent texts, being bleeped. This could be anywhere, the universal time-and-place cancelling urgency of a life-threatening emergency, the relentless, shocked insistence on now. The cold panic.

This is no place for a *flâneur*.

I look across to the shiny reflected panels of glass in the modern office block on the other, northern, side of Euston Road. I am trying to imagine where the famous Adam and Eve Tavern used to be. It is not clear from the old maps which side of the present road it was on and the truth is that it probably sat where some of those traffic islands now help people ford the river of buses, taxis and cars, out where the north end of Tottenham Court Road merges messily with Euston Road. But I like the idea of its being in my patch, on this very corner. There was also an annual Tottenham Court Fair held here until the eighteenth century when the authorities tried to stamp it out because the working classes were becoming too boisterous and disorderly. Eighteenth century lager-louts, they came up Tottenham Court Road, between hedges thick with blackthorn and may blossom, to party at the Adam and Eve. *The Daily Courant* of 22nd July 1727 reported on a case at the Middlesex Quarter Sessions where it was heard that various "common players" had gathered there "to exhibit and act drolls, and use and exercise unlawful games and plays, whereby great numbers of his Majesty's subjects have been encouraged to assemble and meet together, and to commit riots and other misdemeanours... all such players of interludes are deemed and declared rogues and vagabonds" for they "do manifestly and directly tend to the encouragement of vice and immorality, and to the debauching and ruining of servants, apprentices, and others, as well as to the disturbance of the publick peace, by occasioning quarrels, riots and tumults, and other disorders." The Court ordered the High Constable of Holborn Division to "issue forth his precepts to the petty constables of Tattenhoe, alias Tottenhall, alias Tottenham Court"[8] to stop it all. If they had had ASBOs available they would have used them. The authorities seem to have had some partial success in suppressing the actors and the general merriment. A milder annual festival, the Gooseberry Fair, took its place.

What is more affecting than the thought of a lost tavern, the spectral chink of its glasses, especially when, thanks to the slightly puritan attitude of the Bedford Estate, the area is traditionally very poorly supplied with licensed premises? The Adam and Eve was situated on the site of the old Manor House of Totenhale. It had three spacious gardens and a forecourt with large shadowing elm trees, under which were tables and benches for those who preferred to smoke their pipe and take their glass while watching the traffic as it went up and down the New Road (Euston Road) in front of them. One of the highlights for the Adam and Eve regulars was the appearance of the 'Paddington Drag' which stopped once a day at the tavern on its way from Paddington to the City allegedly taking two hours for the trip. Today the 205 bus, on its slow progress to Mile End, makes the journey in a fraction of the time. The pub was famous for its cream teas served in the gardens and in 1628 the poet George Wither in his poem 'Britannia Remembrancer' observed:

> Some to the next adjoining hamlets going.
> And Hogsden, Islington, and *Tottenham Court*,
> For cakes and creame had then no small resorte.

The Adam and Eve was also celebrated for its miniature menagerie consisting of a monkey, a heron, various wild fowl, parrots, and a small pond for goldfish. In 1785 a neighbouring attraction advertised: "Cold Bath, in the New Road, Tottenham Court Road, near the *Adam and Eve* Tea Gardens is now in fine order for the reception of ladies and gentlemen. This bath is supplied from as fine a spring as any in the kingdom, which runs continually through it, and is replete with every accommodation for bathing, situate in the *midst* of a pleasant garden."[9] Its waters were said to be good for people "subject to lowness of spirits and nervous disorders".

I am thinking of the Adam and Eve and its war against "lowness of spirits" because there is a certain bleakness in this windy north western corner of liminal Bloomsbury, a soulless conglomeration of glass and concrete buildings, an urban aridity that needs people, the rough jollity of the Adam and Eve crowd, to enliven it, to humanise it. I also think of the stone mason's yards that were once clustered at this end of Euston Road. Another spectral presence: artisanal Bloomsbury. There is even a PC World behind the A&E building on Tottenham Court Road and where there is a PC World you know where you are on the scale of soullessness.

Moving east, crossing the top of Gower Street, I encounter, at No. 215 Euston Road, the vastness of the Wellcome Research Institution building, a glass and steel stunner built in 2004 by Hopkins Architects. When they demolished the old building, that had been there since it was opened by Henry Wellcome in 1932, I watched its energetic progress as I walked past on my way to Euston Square to get the tube to Paddington, Wales-bound. They simply demolished the whole thing, dug down furiously into the earth, and let this glittering giant Phoenix spring out of the ashes of the old building. Henry Wellcome, whose charitable foundation the Wellcome Trust is the largest charity in the UK, which now shells out £600 million a year – an insight into the staggering profits that drug companies make – was a 'character'. Born in the Wild West in 1853, he ended his life in 1936 as a knight of the realm, amassing a vast collection of historical objects, the Wellcome Collection, and founding a philanthropic empire on the way. Today the Wellcome Building has interesting medical exhibitions, library and research facilities, and a rather comfortable cafe whose attractions have caused the catering contractors recently to put notices on the table reminding people that this is not a library. The Wellcome's permanent exhibition on the first floor has a sometimes scary array of surgical implements, historical sex aids, medical memorabilia and clinical flotsam and jetsam, even a shrivelled Peruvian mummy curled into a tight ball as on the day it was buried.

Euston Road was known simply as the New Road until 1857 and was built (it is said with 100,000 cartloads of gravel) to link Paddington and the City. Around the middle of the eighteenth century, as descriptive accounts of the Adam and Eve suggest, this area was all fields, but an Act of Parliament authorising the construction of a road was passed in the reign of George II in 1756, after bitter battles with the nimbyish Duke of Bedford who thought it came far too close to his town mansion, Bedford House. He should be so lucky. Bedford House was a long way from the sight and sound of the road. Outside my flat the grind of traffic and scream of sirens never stops. Although the Act was passed and the road built (a clause was included prohibiting the erection of buildings within fifty feet of the road which ensured that the houses along its length had generous gardens) there were repeated complaints about the dust and nuisance it would cause. When the railways came during the mid-nineteenth century railway-building frenzy – so vividly described, in the Euston or Somers Town area, just north of Bloomsbury, by Dickens in *Dombey and Son* – the Duke again made sure that no railway terminus was built on his side of the New Road, which is why Euston Road today still feels like a kind of border fence between Bloomsbury and the rest of north London.

EUSTON: THE ENIGMA OF ARRIVAL

For generations of Northerners and Scots this has been their first view of London, coming out of Euston or King's Cross stations. The famous Euston Arch, which many fought to preserve in a campaign led by John Betjeman, vice-President of the Victorian Society, was demolished in 1962. The 1837 arch was seen by its defenders, with its vast, blackened Doric columns, as a symbol of the Railway Age. It formed the grand entrance to the first railway station in the world to be built in a capital city and the first London terminus, a monument of massive significance to the history of the railways. The campaigners cast the destruction of the Arch as: "The Euston Murder". In its place the bleak, unlovely, terminus at Euston – easily London's ugliest and most comfortless, in fact it's impossible to think of a nastier place to find oneself in the capital – remains as the gateway to London for generation after generation of young men and women from the North of England who have come to London to seek their fortune. Or to escape. Or probably both. This is the foundational London myth, of the rude provincial arriving in the capital to make good. Dick Whittington, Will Shakespeare, David Storey (author of *Flight into Camden* (1960)). I myself arrived from Liverpool on a hot late-August day in 1972, on my way to pick hops in Kent, not quite ready to take up permanent residence. I had a couple of hours to spare before my next connection at London Bridge that would take me to the hopfields of Paddock Wood, so I shouldered my rucksack and started walking south, crossing Euston Road into Bloomsbury. Years later, I still cross the raddled remnant of that larger Euston Square that was sliced in two by the building of Euston Road, office blocks standing on the northern part of it where the early nineteenth century 'Nursery Ground' used to stretch back towards Tavistock Square. Its grubbiness never fails to lower the spirits. Opposite the station, the small garden outside the eastern entrance to Friends' House is all that is left of that pastoral side of the former Euston Square.

As an arriving teenager my reactions to Bloomsbury were thoroughly conventional. I noticed the formal, white stuccoed houses in the squares through which I passed (forgetting for the moment that Georgian Liverpool could rival many of them) and formed an immediate impression of an area that had been planned meticulously according to a fierce, if not obsessive, sense of urban geometry. I was not wrong. The Bedford Estate, to this day, retains a strong grip on the built environment of Bloomsbury even if it no longer maintains the six bar gates of the nineteenth century, with gatekeepers in uniform (precursors of the present day high-viz urban policemen and 'community support officers', backed up by CCTV, who monitor to excess every movement of the peaceable residents of this law-abiding faubourg). Undesirables who could not prove their status as true residents of Bloomsbury by showing their silver ticket were turned away by the Duke's heavies and it took legislation, in the end, to force the removal of these barriers. Lodges controlling access to the Bedford Estate were introduced in 1800 and lasted until the new London County Council (LCC) ensured in the London Streets (Removal of Gates) Act of 1890 that the practice would end. The first ones were removed from Woburn Place on 17th October 1891 and the last from Torrington Place in 1893, the year that Gower Street became for the first time a public thoroughfare.

So my first view of Bloomsbury that summer's day turned out to be the correct one: it *is* elegant, spacious, relaxed, still one of the most civilised areas of central London. I continued my walk south and soon realised I was hungry. I stopped at a restaurant that is now the

Yialousa Greek Taverna in Woburn Place but in those days was a cheap chop-house. A slightly less than urbane Scouser, this was the first time I had ever eaten on my own in a public restaurant and I felt, as I placed my order, what countless London arrivals from the North have felt, a mixture of excitement, confusion, gaucheness, and loneliness in the heart of the crowd. I would never have guessed that, nearly three decades later, I would be dividing my life between a house in the Welsh hills and a small flat a few yards from my chop-house, in a block of 1930s flats (what estate agents call 'Art Deco') faintly reminiscent of the Paris apartment block anatomised by Georges Perec in his *Life, A User's Manual.* There are a lot of us in this warren of 500 tiny studio flats – I shall call it Strachey Mansions to protect my neighbours' privacy – the block supervised with formidable efficiency by a former Grenadier guardsman, whom, naturally, I describe affectionately as The Sergeant-Major. From this base, at the exact geometric centre of Bloomsbury, I have operated for a dozen years as the obsessive urban walker mentioned earlier. I have paced every inch of this part of central London. If I am to live in London then this is where I want to be. I can't imagine a better spot – though it is Wales in the end that makes it possible. The city may have a 'buzz' but the heart needs the silent beauty of the Radnor Valley.

After the Wellcome Institute, with its lively café, bookshop, and exhibition galleries, I continue my eastward stroll, crossing the top of Gordon Street and seeing, on my right, Friends' House, the large Quaker hall which has been the site of so many public meetings and political rallies. I first went there for a big National Union of Journalists strike meeting when I worked as a staff journalist on the social services magazine *Community Care* and was, briefly, Father of the Chapel. Subsequently I have seen the giants of Left oratory perform there. Like Tony Benn speaking to legions of the converted and, outside, the gentle snowfall of leaflets and handbills, the dogged newspaper sellers covering every sectarian shade and tint. There is a radical Bloomsbury that connects Friends House, Conway Hall in Red Lion Square (not strictly in my patch), and Camden Town Hall, where I attended, at the time of the invasion of Iraq, an anti-War meeting addressed by, amongst others, the poet Adrian Mitchell giving us yet another rendering of his classic 'To Whom It May Concern' with the refrain: "Tell me lies about Vietnam". I also listened to the plummy accents of theatre director Peter Brook telling us what we already knew, that the powers-that-be were wicked, and we weren't, as we slyly consulted our watches to see if there was going to be time for a pint. There is an older radical tradition in Bloomsbury embodied in individuals like Major Cartwright and other eighteenth and nineteenth century thinkers and activists which I will touch on later. Friends House is also home to The Quaker Centre – another cosy café and a bookshop displaying tempting titles like *Contemporary Social Evils*, a report from the Joseph Rowntree Foundation, and free leaflets on *Quakers Today* and *The Quaker Way*.

And now, on the corner of Upper Woburn Place, I approach St Pancras Church, a massive example (the best of its kind say its advocates) of Greek Revival architecture. A great stone temple with massive caryatids, shaken by the thunderous traffic of the Euston Road. When you pull off the shelves one of those glossy picture books with titles like *London's Churches* usually only this and St George's Bloomsbury get a mention, as if they were the only two Bloomsbury churches in existence.

St Pancras was a 14-year-old Christian martyr, beheaded in 304 AD, at the site marked by the Basilica of Pancratius in Rome. St Pancras Old Church (still sitting behind Euston and King's Cross stations and therefore well outside Bloomsbury) is said to be one of the oldest Christian churches in Britain, though substantial Victorian rebuilding in 1847 more or less obliterated any external sign of its antiquity. It was the pressure of population that led to the building in 1819 of the new St Pancras Church in Bloomsbury. St Pancras parish, originally part of the great forest of Middlesex, was second only to St Marylebone in size in the nineteenth century, covering 27,000 square acres. It included areas like Kentish Town which are well outside the current area and it was, in the nineteenth century, part of the Parliamentary Borough of Marylebone. In 1251, the parish had only 40 houses set in an expanse of farmland and even in 1776 its population was only 600. But by 1911 the population was 218,000. With this increase, boosted considerably in the middle years of the nineteenth century by the railway building boom, came the inevitable urban poverty and destitution. Child-trafficking was a

widespread phenomenon as Walter Brown, a chief clerk in St Pancras borough's cemetery department who became the borough's historian, reported in 1911:

> In the early part of the last century, waggon loads of pauper children might be seen on the country roads on their way to the cotton spinners of Lancashire, to whom they had been apprenticed – or sold into slavery would be the proper term – by the workhouse authorities in London. In close, badly-ventilated, unwholesome factories, wretchedly fed, they were condemned to labour for fourteen or fifteen hours a day. It was the practice of the Directors of the Poor in St. Pancras, whenever there was a sufficient number of these children to be apprenticed, to issue advertisements to that effect. The millowners' agents – ever ready, being paid by commission for each child obtained – immediately approached the Directors, a form of apprenticeship was drawn up, and after receiving a good cheque as bonus from the Directors for taking the children, the agent departed with his cargo to the North. In many instances the children were never heard of again.[10]

Walter Brown's tidy local government officer's soul was appalled by the nineteenth century administration of St Pancras. He described as "terrible" the tangle of 25 different local bodies called Paving Commissioners who were at war with each other, and the loquacious Vestry meetings which were open to all. Eventually things were tidied up and St Pancras parish became, in 1899, a Metropolitan Borough alongside the Borough of Holborn (which collected bits of various other parishes so that between the two they encompassed Bloomsbury). It survived until 1965 when the new London Borough of Camden was formed. As you walk around Bloomsbury today you occasionally see old pre-1965 street signs bearing the name of the Borough of Holborn.

But back to this great church and its fluted Ionic columns and pediments and Grecian ladies with stone beams on their heads. The architect was William Inwood who formed, with his son, Henry, the architectural firm H.W. & W. Inwood, who also designed All Saint's in Kentish Town which, in a nicely circular motion, is now the Greek Orthodox Church. Henry visited Greece in 1819 to study classical Greek architecture at first hand, even taking moulds of the Erectheum, on which some of the St Pancras detail is modelled. The tower was also copied from the Tower of the Winds in Athens. Although described in John Summerson's classic *Georgian London* as "brilliant" and "the queen of early nineteenth century churches",[11] more conservative architects like Pugin, hero of the Gothic Revival, were appalled at this pagan temple in Euston Road. But it remains the earliest and most outstanding example of Greek Revival architecture in London whatever you think of that style.

The church was built to accommodate the local surge in worshippers that accompanied the building-boom for Bloomsbury from the late eighteenth to early nineteenth century. St Pancras Old Church could fit only 150 parishioners and had been outgrown. The New Road (Euston Road) brought a new population and in 1816 an Act of Parliament was procured empowering the Trustees of Old St Pancras to raise £40,000 to build a new church. That sum had doubled three years later and new St Pancras cost £89,000 to build and was the most expensive church in London since St Paul's. It was built of brick faced with Portland stone. There was controversy about the building and at one vestry meeting in the Southampton Tea Gardens three of the vestrymen were arrested in a fracas. Opponents objected to the cost, and wanted to see inherited debts from the old St Pancras workhouse paid off first but they were defeated and on 1st July 1819 the foundation stone was laid in a ceremony presided over by the Duke of York. The next day the *Morning Chronicle* reported on the lively occasion: "When the half of the company had nearly retired, a numerous gang of pickpockets rushed in and went up to the stone where, from the immense pressure of the crowd, they were able more easily to effect their nefarious purposes. A number of ladies were deprived of their shawls, watches, &c; and many gentlemen lost their pocket-books, watch-seals, &c." The actual opening ceremony three years later was more decorous, with many dignitaries and even the Bishops of Llandaff and Bangor having come all the way from Wales for the occasion.

When the caryatids were first made they proved to be too tall and had a nip and tuck, slices taken out of their middles so they would fit. The architect of these was J.F.C. Rossi and he made them of terracotta over an iron core. The six Ionic columns at the far end in the apse were made of scagliola, a mixture of plaster, marble chippings and glue, and the stained glass was by Clayton and Bell. The pulpit and reading-desk are made of the famous Fairlop Oak, which stood in Hainault Forest in Essex, until it was blown down in 1820, and which gave its name to the fair held under its shade. Vaults were built underneath to accommodate 3,000 coffins and these were used, in two world wars, as air-raid shelters. Originally the interior was filled with high oak pews (the expensive ones at the front costing 35 shillings a year) but subsequent restorations and alterations have produced a lighter, less cluttered interior. Until 1953, when it was pulled down, you could see a replica of St Pancras in Old Cape Town Cathedral. Today there is a slight air of shabbiness about the exterior and the churchyard is rather dusty, but it's an excellent place, on Thursday lunchtimes, to sit and listen to the free classical concerts and admire the austere interior, shutting yourself into one of the oak pews with a little door. The parish consists of 6000 residents, a third of whom are estimated to be students, and it declares: "This Church is the spiritual home of a very diverse congregation, which is multi-cultural, multi-racial and of all age groups. Our worship is enriched by visitors from all corners of the world." This is obvious if one stands outside in Upper Woburn Place, watching the world go by.

Continuing eastwards, the towering HQ of the trade union, Unison, is on the right, on the corner of Mabledon Place, not so far away from the largest British union, Unite (born of a merger in 2009 of the Transport & General Workers Union and Amicus), The National Union of Teachers, and several smaller ones. Opposite the British Library are a couple of rare (for Bloomsbury) pubs, the barn-like Euston Flyer (Fullers) and O'Neills the Irish pub. Crossing the top of Judd Street, here is Camden Town Hall, and round the back in Bidborough Street, the Camden Centre where the political meetings take place. This is more or less the boundary between posh or institutional Bloomsbury and the raunchiness of King's Cross. Here used to be a very sleazy district indeed with crack-heads and prostitutes in command of the streets, especially late at night. If I dip into Argyle Street down the side of the public library I am soon in Argyle Square which was once notorious as a red light area but today its hotels (or at any rate a majority of them) have been spruced up and even some international chains like Comfort Inn have taken over premises in the square which, although not particularly comely, seems reasonably safe these days. The trick of the authorities, of course, is simply to export the vice trade and the bad boys somewhere else, and when the grand St Pancras International was relaunched in November 2007 as the Eurostar terminus, the area had to be given a rapid sociological wash and brush-up, sending the *racaille* somewhere to the east. All we are left with is the plain tattiness and scruffiness of the burger bars and tandooris, noodle shops and cheap supermarkets opposite King's Cross Station (which provides their custom) where Euston Road finally merges into the frayed, curving end of Gray's Inn Road, and I have reached the far north-eastern corner of what can conceivably be thought of as Bloomsbury. Good however, to see an old-fashioned, quality business, Franchi's the locksmith and toolstore, still doing business here, between the cafes, one of three showrooms in north London of the operation founded by Guerrino Franchi in 1970.

CARTWRIGHT GARDENS: PHYSICAL JERKS AND WILFRED OWEN

I have a weakness for old guidebooks and histories, which are often as silly and eccentric as those of today but also often informative in surprising ways. Take John Murray's *Handbook to London As it Is* (1879), an early attempt at *Real London.* It begins with a warning: "In no part of the Old World do changes occur so rapidly as in London. An improvement mooted one year is carried into execution the next. The Editor of a Guide-book needs consequently to be ever on the watch, if he desires to place his readers *au courant* with the actual state of things."[12] Now this might sound like common sense but, having lived in Bloomsbury for the past twelve years, what strikes me in fact is how little has changed. A shop disappears here or there – like the wet-fish shop on the corner of Tavistock Place that morphed into Snappy Snaps a week after I moved in. A building is rebuilt, a refurbishment project like the Brunswick makes its mark, but the area isn't *that* different from when I strode into Woburn Place in the early 1970s.

Murray's *Handbook* is full of fascinatingly useless data. In 1879 it reckoned the population of London at 3.5 million, covering 78,000 acres, and helpfully pointed out that this was "more than half the area of ancient Babylon" – just the sort of comparison that I am sure would have occurred to you. What's more, London at this date had 15,000 cows "to fill its milk and cream jugs". There were 8900 public houses, 2000 butchers, 1500 dairy men, 2600 tea dealers and grocers, 3000 boot and shoe makers, 2950 tailors and 700,000 cats "fed by the 3000 horses who die every week", and 90,800 paupers. But the most interesting datum of all was this: "To look after the digestion of this enormous amount of food upwards of 2400 duly licensed practitioners, surgeons and physicians, are daily running to and fro through this mighty metropolis, whose patients, in due course of time and physic, are handed over to the tender mercies of 500 undertakers."

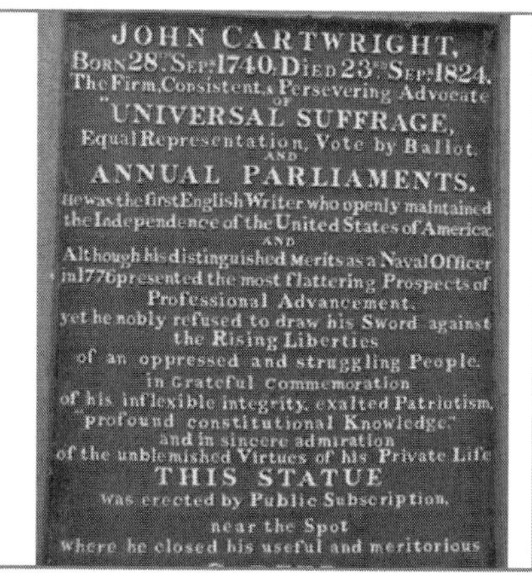

I am now in the mood to explore some more of northern Bloomsbury by retracing my steps along Euston Road in order to drop down into some of the area immediately south of Euston Road. Mabledon Place turns off at Unison HQ and, very soon, on the left, is the National Union of Teachers HQ, Hamilton House (described in *The Buildings of England: London 4: North*, my loyal companion which will be abbreviated henceforth as 'Pevsner', as "Edwardian classical"[13]). I wonder why Bloomsbury has attracted so many of those trade union headquarters I started to describe earlier? Cheaper rents than Westminster but near enough to get at the corridors of power? Handy for the courts? Soon Mabledon Place opens out into the attractive crescent of Cartwright Gardens with its white stuccoed lower floors (mostly hotels) and arched windows, built around 1809-11. This was once known as Burton Crescent, after James Burton, one of the key architect-developers of Bloomsbury but in 1831 it was renamed and a statue was erected in the gardens to Major John Cartwright, the so-called 'Father of Reform', whose progressive virtues are set out in florid prose on a tablet on the plinth. These years at the end of the eighteenth century and the early nineteenth seethed with radical working class protest at home and abroad and some of the Chartist demands that Cartwright backed, like annual parliaments, are as far off realisation as ever. He lived here from 1820-24.

Cartwright Gardens is still a crescent of (mostly) cheaper hotels though a little sprucer than it was when I stayed here in the 1980s on trips to London. These used to be classic British bed and breakfast establishments with shower heads that came off in your hands, a pervasive reek of rising damp, grungy carpets and hideous wardrobes. One of these private hotels was run by an elderly couple who must have long ago retired. It was painted deep green and in the breakfast room we were served on green plates *gigantic* 'full English' breakfasts that would sustain you for a whole day's sightseeing in the capital. During the First World War the gardens (whose tennis courts and benches are currently reserved for the students in the halls of

residence opposite) were requisitioned by the army and used for training purposes. In October 1915, a young volunteer to the Artists' Rifles, whose drill hall was round the corner at No 17 Duke's Road, a building occupied now by The Space modern dance centre, reluctantly submitted himself to the physical jerks discipline of the army sergeant. Wilfred Owen, who was billeted around the corner in 54 Tavistock Square, hated the discipline and dreamed of the relief of off-duty readings and gossip at the Poetry Bookshop in Devonshire Street (see p.116). He wasn't impressed by the prevailing Bloomsbury architectural style: "Tavistock Square is a replica of every other Bloomsbury square; wadded with fog; skeletons of dismal trees behind the palings; but the usual west-end pervasion of ghostly aristocracy."[14]

I swing round and look at the student halls of residence on the east side of Cartwright Gardens, facing the crescent, the Commonwealth Hall and Hughes Parry Hall. Mid-twentieth century buildings bereft of the slightest architectural merit, plain bare windows lacking any decorative detail or design flourish. Rabbit-hutches, or, as one student who lived there once labelled them for me, "hamster-cages". One wonders what kind of commission the 'architect' was given, what lead hung heavily in his or her soul that could result in the churning out of such featureless design in such surroundings. Half way up the wall is a plaque informing the passer-by that Rowland Hill, founder of the modern postal system, lived here from 1837. His neighbour (not granted a plaque) was another nineteenth century innovator, Edwin Chadwick, the sanitary reformer who was responsible for the Public Health Act of 1848.

Between the two quadrants of Georgian terrace a short street leads through westwards to Burton Street, where there are two fine examples of that endangered species, the second hand bookshop. The Marchmont Bookshop at No 39 is a little gem for out-of-print-poetry-buffs and has a very good second-hand stock. Like most traders in this area, however, it seems to hang on by the skin of its teeth. A few doors down at No 45 is another specialist bookshop with a beautifully designed shop-front, the Librairie du Maghreb ("Vous y trouverez l'introuvable") specialising in books on North Africa, the Middle East, Islam and Africa, and run by Mohamed Ben-Madani. It too looks under threat, in spite of the honeyed words of the planners, from the usual toxins: soaring rents and online trading.

Off Burton Street, running west into Upper Woburn Place, is a narrow passageway called Woburn Walk where my way was barred a few years ago by the heavies of a film crew which had taken over to film Orwell's novel *Keep the Aspidistra Flying* (1936), starring Helena Bonham Carter and Richard E. Grant – the story, as it happens, of a young bookseller's assistant. It's not hard to see why film makers would love this little gem of a passage that actually looks a weeny bit like a film-set but has some nice cheap tasty cafés and little galleries. Actually, it is wholly authentic with the bow-fronted shops designed by Thomas Cubitt, another key Bloomsbury architect, around 1822 on the fringe of the Bedford Estate which wanted to keep these traders away from the posh residential streets.

A plaque lets you know that at Woburn Buildings (as it then was called but now No 12 Woburn Walk) the Irish poet W.B. Yeats lived from 1895-1919, keeping a salon on Monday nights. He arrived in Bloomsbury from Dublin and rented one floor from the husband of the charlady of Arthur Symons, the Irish poet and aesthete. He reported that he had a sitting-room: "looking on a raised flagged pavement where no traffic can come – & the bedroom, very small & draughty, looks out on St Pancras Church with its caryatids & trees".[15] Eight years later the novelist Dorothy Richardson moved in opposite and thought the houses "retained something of an ancient dignity, and, with the faded painted ceilings of their main rooms, a touch of former splendour" but they were now a little down at heel. The attic room above Yeats was occupied by a pedlar, an ancient cobbler lived below him and there was a stonemason opposite. A blind beggar stationed himself permanently outside, selling bootlaces and

matches. All that was missing, Yeats observed wryly, was a pawnshop. Pretty as Woburn Walk is, it has still kept this common touch and on a sunny day you can sit in front of Yeats's house eating sausage and chips at one of the café tables. Later, the formidable Lady Gregory would sweep in and impose her influence on Woburn Buildings, providing the poet with a massive leather easy-chair and an interior design suitable for a devotee of the Celtic Revival: "dim blues, tall white paschal candles, walls hung with brown paper, painted furniture, mystic hangings, prints and engravings by Blake, Rossetti, Beardsley".[16] By the time Yeats left in 1919 the floors and woodwork had been painted black and the room hung with orange and, according to one visitor, the poet Ezra Pound, he had "painted the stairs sky blue".[17]

UPPER WOBURN PLACE, OR THE DAY IT ALL WENT VERY QUIET

Emerging from Woburn Walk and turning left into Upper Woburn Place I see on the opposite side of the road a bland block of flats called Endsleigh Court facing the British Medical Association Headquarters. "Ghastly!" was the terse comment of my American friend Rick Mallette, a Professor of English at the University of Chicago, on being asked what it was like to emerge from his temporary apartment at Endsleigh Court on the morning of 7th July 2005. We were sitting at the open air café in Russell Square when we discussed the shocking events of that day which had disrupted his peaceful summer school introducing US students to the world of London theatre. A policeman gave him the grisly advice (before all the scattered body parts had been collected): "Don't look up."

Those of us who live in the busier Bloomsbury thoroughfares are used to noise, but not to the sound of terrorist explosions.

Rattle-rattle-*thump*! Rattle-rattle-*thump*! All day and all night the tourists' wheeled suitcases come and go along the pavements of Woburn Place below my fifth floor studio in Strachey Mansions. At night, as I have said, the traffic never stops except for a faint lessening between roughly 4 and 5 a.m. when, miraculously, the blackbirds start to sing from the plane trees in Russell Square. Shouting and whooping from partying students from the nearby halls of residence, chanting European football fans far from home, midnight choirs of foreign students, singing and clapping in time, demented but

somehow harmless crack-heads, ensure that this is never a quiet street whatever the hour of day or night.

But that day it was different.

On the 7th July 2005 I was working quietly in the Rare Books Room of the British Library, so absorbed that it was some time before I looked up and realised that something wasn't quite right. Why was it so deserted this morning? Why were so few people at their desks, poring, like me, over dusty old volumes. And why, here and there, were groups of people engaged in earnest whispering? I looked up, rather puzzled, until I clicked on the BBC website on my laptop and found the answer. It was confusing at first, just after the bombs went off at 8.50 a.m., only half an hour before I took up my seat in the reading room. Three bombs exploded within fifty seconds of each other on Underground trains and then a fourth, nearly an hour later, in Upper Woburn Place where it meets Tavistock Square, when a bus (that shouldn't have been there because earlier disruption had diverted it from its normal route) was ripped apart. 52 people died in these explosions and 700 were injured. There had, quite simply, never been such an outrage in the entire history of London's transport networks. It was the deadliest attack in London since the Blitz. Not really sure what to do – what could possibly prepare one for such a thing? – I picked up my papers and left the Library. On the streets people were dazed and confused. It was unnaturally quiet. I tried to contact my wife who also worked in Bloomsbury but the mobile phone networks were temporarily switched off. For nearly an hour I wandered about before deciding to try to return home. Strachey Mansions was surrounded by police and fluttering tape. At first I was refused access but later they let me return and eventually the phones were restored and we met up in a café in Holborn still numbed and not yet fully aware from the news bulletins of what exactly had happened and how bad the carnage had been. It would later be confirmed that the third of the bombs had exploded on a southbound Piccadilly Line Underground train travelling between King's Cross and Russell Square. This was one of the deepest of the tube lines and rescue teams worked day and night for several days. We could only get in and out of our flat by ducking under police tapes. The silence continued.

Police, normally only seen racing through the area in cars emitting deafening siren-shrieks, suddenly appeared on the streets and set up a temporary gazebo-style tent at the corner of Russell Square which was much appreciated by tourists seeking directions. There wasn't actually a lot for these police to do, with the result that astonished cyclists engaged in the normal activity of shooting through red traffic lights on pedestrian crossings found themselves for the first time in their lives stopped and given a talking-to by police.

Eventually, of course, we recovered. It was surprisingly fast. A few days, perhaps a week or two, of numbness, of uncertainty, once the Underground at Russell Square was opened, before one risked again sounding its vast depth. Were we afraid? Living in terror of another attack? The fact is that we weren't. At some level one tells oneself that lightning doesn't strike in the same place twice. Pick yourself up. Keep walking. This is not heroism, just common sense. You just keep going because that is all you can do. But I still can't get out of my mind the picture in the *Evening Standard* of a young Muslim woman on her way to work who was blown, senselessly, into pieces. Senseless because this act achieved absolutely nothing for anyone, least of all for Fanon's 'wretched of the earth'. A small plaque on the railings of the BMA headquarters records what happened, and from time to time a passer-by or a tourist stops to read it, before moving on. Contrast this with the emotional atmosphere around ground zero in New York, the way in which St Paul's Church has become wholly converted into a memorial shrine to the 3,000 lost of September 11th 2001, and a new memorial garden is being built on the site of the Twin Towers.

The city never stands still. Its necessary motion is always onward. There is never any time to waste, everyone is in a hurry even if they don't always know where they are going.

The BMA building, outside which the tangled wreckage of the exploded bus sat for at least 48 hours, human blood still perceptible on its walls, is on the site of Tavistock House where Dickens lived from 1851 to 1860, beginning *Bleak House* there in November of 1851. During this decade Dickens, an actor manqué, built himself a theatre in the garden and gave a series of amateur performances in which all the leading parts were played by himself. The play-bills were headed "The Smallest Theatre in the World, Tavistock House".

Bulwer Lytton, William Makepeace Thackeray and Thomas Carlyle were at various times in the audience. Dickens wrote *Hard Times* and *Little Dorrit* here and had many famous visitors including Hans Christian Andersen, who wrote: "In Tavistock Square stands Tavistock House. This and the strip of garden in front of it are shut out from the thoroughfare by an iron railing. A large garden with a grass-plot and high trees stretches behind the house, and gives it a countrified look. In the passage from street to garden hung pictures and engravings. Here stood a marble bust of Dickens.... On the first floor was a rich library with a fireplace and a writing-table, looking out on the garden; the kitchen was underground, and at the top of the house were the bedrooms."[18]

Other residents of Tavistock House have included the radical poet and Chartist, Eliza Cook (1818-1819), the composer Charles Gounod who held singing-classes in the drawing room, and James Perry, editor of the *Morning Chronicle.* In 1860, in the middle of *Great Expectations*, the lease on Tavistock House expired and Dickens moved to Gad's Hill Place in Kent where he lived until his death in 1870. All that is left is a blue plaque on the BMA wall.

Leonard Woolf, husband of Virginia, who lived at No 52 Tavistock Square in the 1920s (destroyed by bombing in 1940 and now the site of the Tavistock Hotel on the square's south side), once led his octogenarian mother out of this north-eastern corner of Tavistock Square to have a look at Woburn Lodge, a building designed around 1824 by William Inwood, architect of St Pancras Church, and situated immediately south of the church but long since demolished. It was now empty and "melancholy" but his mother recalled that "in the road just outside was a turnpike which was only opened to residents in the Square by a ducal retainer who sat in a kind of summer-house next to it. That must have been, I suppose, in the 1860s."[19] This was one of those barriers, already mentioned, that the Bedford Estate used to keep in position to preserve the exclusivity of Bloomsbury until a more democratic era forced their removal at the end of the

nineteenth century.

When Virginia and Leonard Woolf moved into No 52 Tavistock Square on 13th March 1924 (having acquired a ten year lease from the Bedford Estate) it was in large measure because Virginia felt she was vegetating in Richmond where they had been living. If she moved to Bloomsbury, Leonard later reported her as saying: "I might go and hear a tune, or have a look at a picture, or find out something at the British Museum, or go adventuring among human beings." A perfect account of why someone would want to live in Bloomsbury today. The house was a typical Bloomsbury one, built in the early nineteenth century with four storeys and a basement. They put their Hogarth Press into the basement and occupied only the second and third floors because the ground and first floors were already let out to an old-fashioned firm of solicitors, Dollman & Pritchard. The Woolfs stayed there until they moved to Mecklenburgh Square in 1939. In the description of their life in Tavistock Square in the 1920s in his autobiography, Leonard Woolf captures a London quality I have already alluded to:

> I have lived practically all my life in London, but I am again and again surprised by its curious, contradictory character, its huge, anonymous, metropolitan size and its pockets of provincial, almost village life – also the congenital conservatism of Londoners, so that if you scratch the surface of their lives in 1924 you find yourself straight back in 1850 or even 1750 and 1650. In the fifteen years I lived in Tavistock Square I got to know a gallery of London characters who themselves lived in a kind of timeless London and in a society as different from that of Fleet Street, Westminster, Kensington, or Putney – all of which I have known – as Sir Thomas Bertram's in Mansfield Park must have been from Agamemnon's behind the Lion Gate in Mycenae.[21]

Another half a century after those (retrospective) words were written one would not want to quarrel with any of it.

Woolf was thinking, for example, of the foul-mouthed Dickensian character, Mrs Giles, who cleaned the solicitor's offices at night and who lived in an attic around the corner in Marchmont Street. Leonard was fond of taking his dog for a walk in Tavistock Square and became a member of the committee running the Square. By-laws dating back to 1840 stipulated that only householders around the Square had access to it with a key, a tradition that exists today only in Bedford and Mecklenburgh Squares, all the others having long ago permitted public access. Other by-laws stipulated that no servants should be allowed to desecrate Tavistock Square by stepping out in it and children's games were also regulated. In control of all this was the Square keeper, a man who knew everything that happened in his Bloomsbury patch (more or less co-terminous with the area I am covering) and probably very little beyond it.

At the back of No 52 was a large former billiard room now used as a storeroom for the Hogarth Press "and there embedded among the pyramids and mountains of parcels, books, and brown paper sat Virginia with her disembowelled chair, her table, and her gas fire".[22] The author of *A Room of One's Own* had found her place to write. Alas, however, her sleep was disturbed by the scampering and scurrying of rats displaced by the clearing of land for a massive building project behind them, the Royal National Hotel, constructed by the Imperial Hotel Group, and which runs the entire length of Woburn Place from Tavistock Square to Russell Square to the south (forming the view from my window as I write). The rats were eventually defeated with the help of an LCC rat-catcher but then there was building noise during the construction and when the hotel was finished late night jazz bands in the ballroom facing their sitting room window caused Leonard and Virginia to take legal action. Fearful of the Bedford Estate as their landlord (and aware of its keenness to grant more land to the Imperial Group and consequent reluctance to encourage any criticism of the hoteliers from leaseholders who knew their fate was in the Duke of Bedford's hands) most of the residents were reluctant to help, so the Woolfs went it alone, using the solicitor in the rooms below, and won. The hotel had to close all the windows of the ballroom if a band was playing and all Leonard's legal costs were paid. This story has lost none of its resonance as, even today, residents battle against the noise created by the hotels, restaurants and bars and their roistering patrons who, perhaps understandably, find it difficult to conceive of central Bloomsbury as a place where people might want to sleep like suburban commuters preparing for the next day at the office.

Tavistock Square, laid out in 1824, has the gardens at its centre and at the centre of these the squatting figure of Mahatma Gandhi, whose presence has attracted a small scattering of peace memorials over the years, a bitter irony given the thirteen fatalities of July 2005. In 1994 a Conscientious Objectors' Stone was unveiled by Sir Michael Tippett, president of the Peace Pledge Union, and there is a nearby flowering cherry tree commemorating the victims of

Hiroshima. The Gandhi statue (he studied law at nearby University College which explains the choice of site) was unveiled in May 1968 by the then Prime Minister, Harold Wilson, to the sound of barracking by a local politico who wanted the money to have been spent on the needy people of Bloomsbury. Another important memorial is that, in the south-eastern corner of the Square, to Lousia Aldrich-Blake (1865-1925), the first woman in Britain to qualify as a surgeon. Not far away in Hunter Street is the site of the Women's Royal Free Hospital where she and Elizabeth Garrett Anderson (founder of the women's hospital in her name) and Sophia Jex-Blake (founder of the London Medical school for Women) all worked when the male-dominated institutions excluded them. Both the Woolfs have memorials, the most recent being a small bust of Virginia in the north-west corner of the square.

Tavistock Place runs eastwards from the south-east corner of Tavistock Square and on the street's northern side is Mary Ward House, formerly the Passmore Edwards Settlement founded by Mary Augusta Ward, the novelist 'Mrs Humphry Ward', granddaughter of Thomas Arnold the famous headmaster of Rugby school and butt of Lytton Strachey's elegant mockery in *Eminent Victorians*. Mary Ward House (which these days houses the National Institute for Social Work) was built in 1895 and has all the art nouveau period flavour of that decade. Its high moral purpose (connected to Marchmont Hall nearby in Marchmont Street which once provided facilities and activities for the deserving poor who were in plentiful supply in Bloomsbury's back streets) makes it my first example of what I call Worthy Bloomsbury. It was one of countless austere institutions of the nineteenth century through which highly educated people of Christian or Humanist bent ministered in various ways to the material, moral and intellectual needs of their social inferiors. The interesting and attractive architecture of Mary Ward House helps to offset all this well-bred worthiness. Mary Ward was a strong advocate of improving education for children with disabilities and of providing

play facilities for children, which goes some way to balancing her passionate opposition to women's suffrage. She was the first President of the Anti-Suffrage League in 1908, fighting the movement to give women the vote. During the 1880s she lived at 61 Russell Square but the site is now buried under the Imperial Hotel.

Today the Mary Ward Centre in Queen Square is an adult education centre that bears her name. Tavistock Place today consists mostly of offices (including those of the Poetry Book Society) and a row of rather shabby cheap hotels and staff houses for the Imperial Hotel Group. There is even a Welcome Inn that predates the chain of that name. Crossing Marchmont Street, Compton Place, a little alleyway off to the left, leads to The Generator, a funky-looking hostel much favoured by foreign students and backpackers. In spite of the presence of large numbers of young people in Bloomsbury – as students and patrons of the numerous halls of residence – funkiness is not a quality much in evidence. Worthy Bloomsbury, together with academic and institutional Bloomsbury, tends to win out. Students, outside their college bars and one or two pubs, probably go elsewhere to party, to Soho and the West End, or northwards to Camden Town for more illicit recreational substances. Like some migrating species of bird, the foreign students arrive in Bloomsbury around the week before Easter. Sometimes up to a hundred of them progress along the streets from The Generator or the big hotels of the Imperial Group or halls of residence let out in the academic holidays towards the British Museum and other mandatory sights: noisy, chattering, tightly packed crocodiles, forcing the locals to step aside into the gutter.

Tavistock Place ends at Hunter Street and, turning left this becomes Judd Street running north to Camden Town Hall and Euston Road again. These are the scruffy streets of northern Bloomsbury with their tandooris and launderettes, late night mini-markets, computer-repair shops, and pubs, that a Georgian terrace or two can hardly redeem. The Internet Café in Judd Street has an interesting

display of hubble-bubble pipes in the window but I have never seen them in use by customers, and the Skinners' Arms (commemorating the Skinners' Company which owned so much of the land around here) a few doors down is one of Bloomsbury's best pubs, with good real ale and an interior full of stained glass and late Victorian detail. They also do a good plate of fish and chips so that those who have just got off the Eurostar can tick two tourist boxes right away: 'a typical British pub' and 'typical British fish and chips' within five minutes of arrival. Off Judd Street, however, in Leigh Street, the North Sea Fish Bar has the best proper fish and chips in the area and is always said to have been the favourite of the former miner's leader, Arthur Scargill, a loyal customer when in town. A newly trendy restaurant for youth, especially Chinese youth, in Leigh Street is Chilli Cool Sichuan Cuisine. Next door is another second-hand bookshop specialising in rare limited editions. A first edition of Virginia Woolf's Hogarth Press *The Waves* with an immaculate jacket sits patiently with a price tag of £800. I once stopped to rummage in a trough of books not normally set up outside the shop and had my collar felt by a young woman with a clipboard and headset. She pointed out behind her a film crew I had contrived not to notice until then, and explained that the book-trough was from the props department and they were shooting and would I just get along. Sharpish. Random film crews seem to be a hazard of Bloomsbury life.

PASSING THROUGH

The Imperial Group, which runs six massive hotels in Bloomsbury, is a major employer as well as a major visual presence in Bloomsbury and the principal reason why there are so many tourists about. The Walduck family, who still own the group, are worth £70 million according to *The Times* 'rich list', but they are an elusive dynasty and hard to document. For many people, therefore, Bloomsbury is a place of transience – for nothing is more transient than work in 'the hospitality industry': seasonal, uncertain, short-term. I once worked in a hotel in Ireland for the summer and, towards the start of September, I was an old hand, having seen many staff come and go. Squashed into staff houses and hostels adorned with notices about having no parties, or making too much noise or having guests, lonely in a strange bed in a strange city, the hotel workers will have a different perspective on Bloomsbury from the *flâneurs*, academics, celebrity residents like Ricky Gervais and Alexei Sayle. Add them to the floating tourist population, and the students passing through for three years at most on average, and you have a sort of two-tier population of Bloomsberries. Probably the stable population of residents in mansion blocks, or public housing estates is a minority. The majority is in flux. I ask myself, as I walk around the patch, what this means to the sense of identity of an area and its sense of community. Bloomsbury *is* a real place, with a real identity, yet most of the people who pass me on the street are passing through, passing on. They have no stake in the idea of permanence. But I am forgetting the traders, and office workers, and professionals whose Bloomsbury is as real as mine, who spend their days here, and the regular visitors, the British Museum buffs, the researchers and scholars, the people-up-for-meetings, the hospital patients, the shoppers, the drinkers and diners. They all have their Bloomsbury, their idea, their take. And it belongs to us all.

Footnotes

1. Henry James, *Collected Travel Writings* (New York, Library of America, 1993) 'English Hours' p36. Original edition 1888
2. V.S. Pritchett, *London Perceived* (1986) p168
3. Ford Madox Ford, *The Soul of London* (1905) Everyman edition 1995, p7
4. Ibid, p6
5. Ibid., p4
6. Quoted by John Strype (1720) in his revised edition of John Stow's 1698 *Survey of London*, p32
7. *The Times*, 27th November 1933, p10. The best historical introduction to Bloomsbury is Eliza Jeffries Davis' book-length article, 'The University Site, Bloomsbury' in *London Topographical Record*, Vol XVII, 1936
8. Samuel Palmer, *St Pancras: being Antiquarian, Topographical, and Biographical Memoranda, relating to the Extensive Metropolitan Parish of St. Pancras, Middlesex* (1870), p196-7
9. Ibid., p206
10. Walter Brown, *St Pancras Open Spaces and Disused Burial Grounds* (1911), p87
11. John Summerson, *Georgian London* (1945) p200
12. *Handbook to London As It Is* (1879, new edition revised) John Murray, p5

13. Bridget Cherry and Nikolaus Pevsner, *The Buildings of England: London 4: North* (1998), p330
14. *Wilfred Owen: selected letters*,edited by John Bell (1985), p167
15. Roy Foster, *W.B.Yeats: A Life. I. The Apprentice Mage* (1997), p161
16. Ibid., p 187
17. Roy Foster, *W.B.Yeats: A Life. II. The Arch-Poet* (2003), p83
18. Cited by E Beresford Chancellor in *The History of the Squares of London: Topographical and Historical* (1907) p244
19. Leonard Woolf, *Sowing: An Autobiography of the Years 1880-1904* (1960), p6
20. Leonard Woolf, *An Autobiography 2: 1911-1969* (1980), p272. Originally *Downhill All the Way* (1967)
21 .ibid, p274
22. ibid, p223

CENTRAL

Today I have decided to proclaim, unilaterally, the centre of Bloomsbury. I haven't actually got out a pair of school compasses and drawn a circle touching the four sides of my wonky rectangle but it seems to me that the Bar Centrale, quite apart from its name, is as good a place as any for the bull's eye and, better still, no one else has ever suggested it. In Bernard Street, next to Russell Square Underground Station, the Bar Centrale is the Siamese twin of the Italian restaurant next door, La Bardigiana. It's a cheerful, lively, 'typical' Bloomsbury Italian café, more intimate than the ones scattered near the British Museum, and does a nice home made broccoli soup and bread for only £2.50, out-staring the pricier and more crowded upstart Pret à Manger chain on the opposite side of the street. A good place to sit and pick up and finish the thread of Bloomsbury history I left ticking over earlier with the gift of the Bloomsbury Manor by Henry VIII in 1545 to his Lord Chancellor, Sir Thomas Wriothesley, who became, two years later, the first Earl of Southampton.

This is a book about the living Bloomsbury, but history shaped it and what one sees doesn't make complete sense without knowing how we got here, so I intend to finish the story as far as 1800, after which I will merely make occasional allusions to the past as required.

The Earl of Southampton already had a town house in London, in Holborn, called Southampton House, at Holborn Bars, so he had no need to move into his new Bloomsbury Manor, hidden from view behind the line of new houses along Holborn, its lands stretching northwards with a raggedy boundary line caused by the historical accumulation of parcels of land. It was farmland, dotted with ponds, and there was an actual manor house with two gables and a drive leading up to it from Holborn that is shown in sixteenth century maps, near to a bit of land called Pond Piece. Since he had his own grand house, the Lord Chancellor let the Bloomsbury Manor House and the land behind it called Long Field or, as some called it later, The Long Fields. This was profitable letting and the rustic life of

Bloomsbury, with grazing sheep and haymaking, continued as it had in the days when the Carthusian monks owned the land, until the third decade of the seventeenth century. In the reign of Henry II the historian Fitzstephen had written: "a great forest stood to the north of the city, extending towards Hampstead and Highgate, in which were store of wild beasts.... In the north suburb are the houses and gardens of the citizens, watered by divers rivulets, full, pleasant, and clear, and often turning mills with a sprightly noise. The adjacent land is not of an hungry mould, but as the fruitful fields of Asia, abounding in corn and wine."[1]

The Earls of Southampton during these years had their ups and downs. The third Earl, Henry, known for being Shakespeare's patron, had his estates confiscated because he took part in the rebellion of the Earl of Essex and as a result the Bloomsbury rents were paid between 1601 and 1603 to the Crown. But with the accession of James I things started looking up again and by the time the Earl died in 1624 houses had pushed out right along Holborn to St Giles, making his successor, the fourth Earl, resolve to sell off Southampton House, demolish it, and carve up the site for lucrative building plots. The building boom had been steadily reducing his amenities anyway, so the idea of building a new house in the quieter Bloomsbury fields, or upgrading the Manor, looked like a good idea. However, the Privy Council, with its policy of restricting London's growth, initially refused him permission to build and it was not until 1638 that he got the Letters Patent allowing him to pull down Southampton House and liberate the housing land.

At this time the Bloomsbury Manor House was leased to a William Payne, described as "a citizen and salter"[2] and surrounded by orchards and gardens. Along Holborn the houses shared the street frontage with a blacksmith's forge called The Horseshoe and an inn called The Crane, and there were many market gardens selling produce but also providing nursery trees and shrubs for the grand new houses being built along Holborn. The famous Bloomsbury Cherry Orchard was a landmark as well as a buffer against the builders, and the more westerly part of the estate was leased to William Short (whose name is remembered in Short's Gardens). Short was a gardener whose Licours, or Liquorice Garden, between today's Bury Street and Coptic Street specialised in growing medicinal herbs. The Fourth Earl, once he had obtained building permission, decided to construct a new house in the Long Field behind the old manor house rather than refurbish the latter, but the death of his wife in 1640 and the outbreak of Civil War put all these plans on hold. The only building that actually took place was of two batteries and a breastwork across the Long Field (roughly where the south side of Russell Square is today) as part of a defensive network across London to keep out the Royalist forces. In 1646 the Earl had to pay the victorious Parliamentary forces a fine of £6,466, estimated as one tenth of his total assets. This was such a setback that he retired to the country estate of the Southampton family at Titchfield until about 1657 when he once again revived the idea of his Bloomsbury mansion. The Privy Council told him to build it of brick and stone rather than combustible wood, and it consisted of one long central block with two short wings and was initially known as Southampton House in the Fields. The boundary of the garden at the rear was the remnant of the Parliamentary fort whose mound was used to create a raised terrace walk.

On 2nd October 1664, Samuel Pepys wrote in his *Diary* a description of "Lord Southampton's new buildings in the fields" which occupied bits of Pond Piece, the Licours Garden, the great Cherry Garden and part of the Long Field. And on 9th February 1665 the diarist John Evelyn: "dined at my Lord Treasurer's, the Earle of Southampton, in Bloomsbury, where he was building a noble square or Piazza, a little towne; his owne house stands too low, some noble roomes, a pretty cedar chapel, a naked garden to the North, but good aire."[3] This "little towne" was the beginnings of Bloomsbury Square, which grew up after 1665 in front of Southampton House and the "good aire", which everyone noticed, blew in from the Hampstead and Highgate hills to the north across the Earl's rear gardens – but the house, of course, faced firmly south towards the City, Holborn and the Strand. The housing market in Bloomsbury was starting to take off as city merchants decided that they wanted to live outside the cramped and crowded City and many houses, both large and small, were built and roads started to be made. In January 1662 the Earl had managed to get a licence to hold a market on Tuesdays, Thursdays and Saturdays but various writers seem to have concluded that Bloomsbury Market was a bit of a washout. John Strype, who in 1720 updated the 1698 *Survey* of London by John Stow, observed that: "*Bloomsbury-market* is a long Place, with two Market-Houses, the one for Flesh, and the other for Fish; but of small account."[4] The Market was situated around the south-west corner of today's Bloomsbury Square roughly where the Swedenborg Society building now stands, Barter Street at its side being the approach road.

The Great Plague of London had naturally created interest in healthful living and doctors were now arguing for more space and amenity in houses. In 1665 Dr Everard Maynwaringe in his *Morbus Polyrhizos et Polymorphaeus: A Treatise of the Scurvy* discussed the melancholia or hysteria associated with the scurvy. He recommended the air of Bloomsbury as a cure for scurvy. There was not much scientific evidence but it probably helped the Earl's property development. The Doctor wrote:

> And here I cannot but take notice of Bloomsbury (the Right Honourable Earl of Southampton's property and seat) for the best part about London, both for health and pleasure exceeding other places. It is the best air and the finest prospect, being the highest ground, and overlooking other parts of the city. The fields bordering upon this place are very pleasant and dry grounds for walking and improving of health. A fit place for nobility and gentry to reside in that make their abode about London, there being the country air, pleasure and city conveniences joined together; now lately improved and built upon, and still increasing with fair and well contrived buildings, a good addition and ornament to this place.[5]

On 14th May 1667, the Fourth Earl of Southampton, Thomas Wriothesley, died and his three daughters met to parcel up his many estates. They decided to cast lots. His second daughter, Rachel (childless widow of Lord Vaughan) received some land in Hampshire but most importantly "Southampton House and the manors of Bloomsbury and St Giles in Middlesex". Two years later she married William Russell (second son of William, Fifth Earl of Bedford) on 31st July 1669 at Titchfield in Hampshire. After her first marriage at the age of 17, this second marriage was a love match. She was aged 33 and her new husband was 29. Her mother, widow of the Fourth Earl, was not quite ready, however, to vacate Southampton House, hanging on until March 1669 when she and Rachel signed an agreement that she would go.

1669 is another of those key dates in the history of Bloomsbury for it marks the acquisition of the Bloomsbury Estate by the Russell family. They haven't let go ever since. In that year Southampton House in the Fields was earning around £2000 a year from its farming tenants and in 1670 Russell Street was built to connect the house to what was then Tottenham Court Lane. When Rachel's stepsister Elizabeth married the Earl of Montagu they built a house west of Southampton House in Baber's Field called Montagu House, on whose site the British Museum would eventually stand. The architect was Robert Hooke. The Earl of Thanet also built Thanet House around this time. These three grand houses formed the centre of emerging Bloomsbury, along the line of what is now Great Russell Street, and north of which the fields would remain for another century. Strype confirms the importance of this cluster of aristocratic mansions in the fields:

> *Great Russell-street*, a very handsome, large and well-built Street, graced with the best Buildings in all *Bloomsbury*, especially the north Side, as having Gardens behind the Houses, and the Prospect of the pleasant Fields up to *Hampstead* and *Highgate*. This Street takes its Beginning at *King's-street*, and runs westward into *Tottenham-road*, being of great Length, and, in its Passage, faces *Bedford-house*, *Montague-house*, and *Thanet-house*: But, for Stateliness of Building and curious Gardens, *Montague-house* hath the Pre-eminence, as indeed of all Houses within the Cities of *London* and *Westminster*, and the adjacent Parishes.[6]

Unfortunately, the new Russell era ended in tragedy for Rachel when William, who was made Lord Russell in 1678, became embroiled in 'The Popish Plot' and backed the wrong side. He was publicly executed on 21st July 1683 in Lincoln's Inn Fields by the notorious hangman, Jack Ketch. Lady Rachel Russell was desolate, writing on 1st Oct 1684 after living in Woburn for a year after the death of her husband, about her plans to return to Southampton House: "I have to acquaint you with my resolve to try that desolate habitation of mine at London, this winter. The doctor agrees it is the best place for my boy, and I have no argument to balance that; nor could I take the resolution to see London till that was urged; but by God's permission, I will try how I can endure that place – in thought, a place of terror to me!"[7] She lived on in Southampton House as a widow and when her father in

law, the Earl of Bedford, was created Duke of Bedford and Marquess of Tavistock in 1694 her son Wriothesley became Lord Tavistock and inherited Bedford House in the Strand, where he lived until it was demolished in 1705. He died of smallpox in 1711 aged 32 but not before he had made the grand tour and imported Italian architectural influence into Southampton House (which, to confuse matters, now started to be called Bedford House). By the time of the Fourth Duke and Duchess of Bedford in 1732 the area in front of the house was popularly known as Southampton Square (though as early as 1703 it had also been referred to as Bloomsbury Square). In the mid-eighteenth century, therefore, the area around Bloomsbury Square and Great Russell Street, Southampton Street (now Southampton Row) and King Street (now Coptic Street) was still the core of fashionable Bloomsbury. But it remained rural outside this residential core. The poet Thomas Gray, who lived in lodgings in Southampton Row, wrote to his friend William Palgrave on 24th July 1759:

> I am now settled in my new territories commanding Bedford Gardens, and all the fields as far as Highgate and Hampstead, with such a concourse of moving pictures as would astonish you; so *rus-in-urbe-ish*, that I believe I shall stay here, except little excursions and vagaries, for a year to come. What though I am separated from the fashionable world by broad St Giles's, and many a dirty court and alley, yet here is air and sunshine, and quiet, however, to comfort you: I shall confess that I am basking with heat all summer, and I suppose shall be blown down all the winter, besides being robbed every night; I trust, however, that the Museum, with all its manuscripts and rarities by the cart-load, will make ample amends for all the aforesaid inconveniences.[8]

In spite of Gray's reference to the seediness to the west, vividly etched by his contemporary Hogarth in 'The Rookery of St Giles' (see p.96), it is still the rurality of central and northern Bloomsbury that strikes him. In that same year, 1759, the Duke's records show that three shillings were paid to two labourers for sitting up all night "to watch the fat cattle in Bedford House paddock" [that paddock being Gray's 'Bedford Fields', meaning probably the area behind Bedford House that is now Bedford Place leading north to Russell Square]. Sheep and cattle were regularly brought by drovers from Woburn, a two day journey, broken at Bedford and Colney, with the stock being pastured on the Bloomsbury paddocks for a short time before ending up at Smithfield.

THE TERRIBLE SHEARS: THE CAPPERS' FARM

One of the Duke's eighteenth century tenants was Christopher Capper, described in his obituary as "a great Cow-keeper" whose farmhouse at 195 Tottenham Court Road (now the site of Heal's) was inherited by his formidable daughters the Miss Cappers, the scourge of the Bloomsbury yobs. They rented most of the Duke's fields north of Great Russell Street, complaining to his agent when the butchers of Bloomsbury Market tried to introduce their own sheep into the fields. The pair were convinced that all sorts of anti-social behaviour was rife in the fields, with their winding paths where the locals flew kites and bathed in the ponds. Sometimes the Cappers went on freelance moral cleansing rides on horseback, in riding habits and wearing men's hats, the elder of the two, Miss Esther, on an old grey mare, snipping kite strings with a pair of large shears, stealing the clothes of naked bathers, and chasing courting couples and canoodlers out of the long grass. Esther, and her sister Mary Booth, stirred up a vigorous local vigilante spirit as one contemporary report indicates, in which a zealous citizen complains to the Duke of Bedford about the state of things in Southampton Row and the fields and "the vile rabble of idle and disorderly people, who assemble there to play at cricket, and such like pastimes, to the no small danger, and hurt, of the harmless people, who either walk for air or business." Warming up, the anonymous objector went on: "Another nuisance of a most shameful nature I shall speak to, and that is running races, almost stark naked, and some quite so, which is shocking in a civilized country, and calls for the speediest remedy. But such abandoned miscreants can never be reclaimed, without a severe execution of the laws, and some examples made; such wretches are not to be borne, indulgence does but augment the mischief, nothing Sir but the whip, or battoon, that is the cudgel will do with the vulgar."[9] On 10th June 1766 the *Daily Gazeteer* reported that the High Constable of Holborn found in the fields on a Sunday in June: "upwards of two hundred and fifty dog-fighters, bullies, chimney sweepers and sharpers all assembled and at work. As soon as he and his officers entered the ring... they set their mastiff dogs at them, who had more humanity than their brutal masters."[10] Today's capering and mumbling winos and addicts, pavement-riding teenage cyclists, or binge-drinking students are a poor continuance of this tradition of Bloomsbury

mayhem but the backchat and sarcastic 'have-a-nice-days' of disappointed *Big Issue* sellers or Russell Square charity muggers echo the eighteenth century complaint that fruit and vegetable hawkers in the fields were "abusive" when their produce was declined.

Esther Capper was at the forefront of opposition to the construction of The New Road (Euston Road) and backed the campaign against it led by the Duke of Bedford. She wrote to him in 1756:

> My Lord,
> I am informed of a Road intended to be made at the Back of Your Grace's Estate, which, from the Dust and Number of People, must entirely spoil those Fields, and make them no better than one common land.
>
> I most humbly intreat your Grace to prevent such an Evil, for it will be impossible for me to hold your Grace's Estate without a large abatement of Rent.[11]

Between the Capper's Farm (which survived as a building until 1917) and the King's Head Inn further north at the Tottenham Court Road turnpike – vividly portrayed by Hogarth in his picture, 'The March of the Guards to Finchley' (1750), which is the pride of the Thomas Coram collection in Bloomsbury – there was little else but open fields. As well as working-class bacchanale these lent themselves to duelling and duck-shooting and it was here that the curious legend of the Field of the Forty Footsteps – once the best-known of Bloomsbury legends – had its origin in the previous century. According to the legend, in 1692 two brothers in love with the same woman challenged each other to a duel. The young woman watched from a bank as they each took twenty paces and fired. Both died instantly. It was said that grass never grew again on the duelling ground. For another 100 years the legend of the Field of the Forty Footsteps (sometimes known as the legend of the Brothers' Steps) brought sightseers to Bloomsbury, including the 77 year old John

Wesley who regarded the footsteps "with awe as 'marks of the Lord's hatred of duelling'."[12] The seventeenth century biographer and gossip John Aubrey records in his *Miscellanies* yet another legend in exactly the same place, the fields behind what is now the British Museum:

> The last summer, on the day of St. John the Baptist (1694), I accidentally was walking in the pasture behind Montague House; it was 12 o'clock. I saw there about two or three-and-twenty young women, most of them well-habited, on their knees very busie, as if they had been weeding. I could not presently learn what the matter was; at last a young man told me, that they were looking for a coal under the root of a plantain to put under their heads that night, and they should dream who would be their husbands. It was to be found that day and hour.[13]

In the nineteenth century many of these fields were divided by turnstiles and through them ran the water pipes of the New River Company, propped up in places to the height of six or eight feet, so that people could walk under them to gather the renowned water-cresses which grew there in great abundance. But this bucolic ground was doomed and towards the end of the eighteenth century it was finally swallowed up by the pressure of development. The last quarter of the century, marked by the start of the building of Bedford Square in 1775 by the fifth Duke of Bedford, saw the final extinction of the Long Field as construction began north of Great Russell Street. The new development sounded the keynote of Bloomsbury development: space (20 of the 112 acres of the Bedford Estate were to be gardens). The architectural distinction, elegance, and the overall sense of coherent, unified design that comes from a single landowner commissioning various builders and architects were now what Bloomsbury was all about.

RUSSELL SQUARE OR WHO STOLE THE TURKISH BATHS?

Coming out of the Bar Centrale it is a minute's walk westwards to Russell Square, the largest of Bloomsbury's squares, but just behind the block in which the bar is situated is the famous Horse Hospital which has become recently a favoured hip venue for book launches

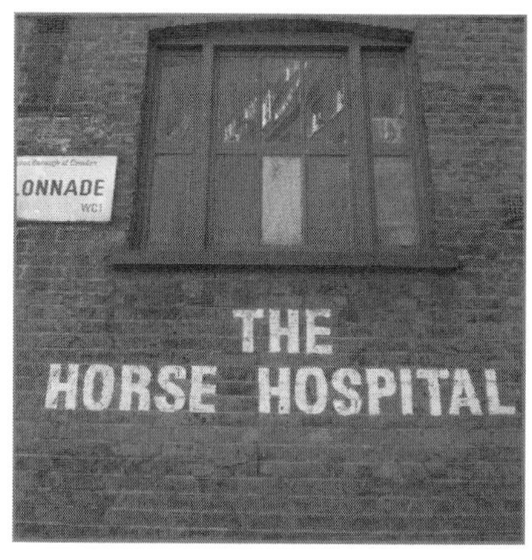

by small independent publishers, including my own Rack Press poetry imprint. Our most recent launch, in 2010, attracted a good crowd in the subdued cellar light, with the poetry editor of the *Times Literary Supplement*, Alan Jenkins, standing on the cobbles with veteran poet and critic, Alan Brownjohn, listening to poets Katy Evans-Bush, Philip Morre and Ian Parks. But we were occupying a space usually given over to more avant-garde happenings under the Chamber of Pop Culture banner. The Horse Hospital, a former infirmary for sick cab horses, in use until the First World War, was taken over by Roger Burton, a costume designer, to hold The Contemporary Wardrobe Collection, his exhibition of film and theatre costumes. In the 1970s Roger helped to design the famous shop in King's Road run by Vivian Westwood and Malcolm McLaren and today the Horse Hospital is also a venue for avant-garde pop music, films and art exhibitions. It is situated in The Colonnade which runs parallel to Bernard Street along the back of Russell Square Underground, a fascinating little mews street of cobblestones, nestling quietly behind the bustle of the tourist crowds. Built in 1797 by James Burton, the Horse Hospital was rebuilt in the 1860s and its interior is dramatic, with sloping cobbled ramps going down to the cellar area where events take place, and where the cast iron pillars and original tethering rings create a special atmosphere.

Russell Square is dominated on its eastern side by the massive 1890s Russell Hotel in red brick and terracotta (bits of which seem to have been left over by the builders and stuck, here and there, with varying degrees of success, on some of the white stucco fronts of the houses in the Square). It's a massive structure, like a crazily excessive French chateau, but you can't miss it or mistake it for anything else. In its time it had a slightly questionable reputation but today it is perfectly respectable – and expensive. It was here that a publisher on the other side of the square, T.S. Eliot, brought his secretary, Valerie Fletcher, thirty years his junior, for drinks after work, sometimes presenting her with red roses. She became the second Mrs Eliot. Some

unpublished fragments for *Old Possum's Book of Practical Cats* refer to the Hotel. On the original site were ordinary houses lived in during the nineteenth century by, amongst others, the suffragette Emmeline Pankhurst, a youthful Edgar Allan Poe and F.D. Maurice, the founder of Christian Socialism, who would rise at 6 a.m. every morning, take a cold bath, then proceed to dictate to the unfortunate Mrs M, all day long, thousands of words of his worthy tracts on social improvement until he was ready for a frugal dinner at 6.30. At the same epoch, the Square (like Bedford Square to the west) was popular with lawyers, journalists and actors. It was in Russell Square that Becky Sharp, heroine of Thackeray's *Vanity Fair*, was introduced to the Sedleys not long after the Square was first laid out in 1800. Italo Svevo stayed here in the 1920s on a business trip and lamented the rise of the automobile which, since he first came to London around the turn of the century (staying in Turner's guest house at No 46 Woburn Place where he was given "a splendid room, and excellent lunch and an exquisite dinner"[14]) had displaced the cab and filled the air with the scent of petrol. Also along Woburn Place was Bogey's Bar, painted by a precocious 17 year old Patrick Heron but long since vanished.

In the north-west corner of Russell Square, a small brown Camden Council plaque records the fact that Faber and Faber was once based at No 24 and that its Poetry Editor T.S. Eliot worked in what is now known as The Faber Building from 1925 to 1965. His deranged first wife, Vivienne Haigh-Wood, used to push bars of chocolate through the letterbox, imagining him to be starving and imprisoned inside. He later wrote: "To her, the marriage brought no happiness. To me, it brought the state of mind out of which came *The Waste Land*."[15] Faber and Faber, after moving to a concrete box in Queen Square, are currently back in a more elegant building on the corner of Great Russell Street and Montague Street. Bloomsbury has always been popular with publishing houses (often quite literally houses,[16] the social stratification implicit in their eighteenth century design fitting perfectly the élitist world of gentlemanly mid-twentieth century

British publishing: accounts department in the basement, bosses elegantly disporting themselves in the first floor drawing room, junior staff pigeon-holed in the more constrained upper floors, caretaker in the attic). Faber's caretaker, Mr Tansley, who had been poisoned by mustard gas in the First World War, lived with his wife in the attic at No 24, and used to serve lunch of meat and two veg to the directors in the boardroom every Wednesday.

Opposite the Faber Building is one of London's thirteen remaining cabmen's shelters (it was originally sited in Leicester Square), a green building like a super-sized Tardis that still serves tea and snacks to the taxi trade (recently extending its menu to cover Thai dishes – a shock to the souls of deceased cabmen). Don't even think of gatecrashing if you don't possess a taxi driver's badge. The shelters were originally provided by the Cabmen's Shelter Fund, a charity founded by the Earl of Shaftesbury in 1874 ostensibly to give cabmen 'wholesome' food but really to keep them out of the pubs. Between 1875 and 1914 a total of 61 shelters were erected, with the police stipulating that they should take up no more space on the public highway than a horse and a cab.

In 2002, almost exactly 200 years after its construction, Russell Square was given a facelift and the original landscaping of Sir Humphrey Repton, its horseshoe paths and lime tree walks and tasteful railings (the originals having been melted down, pointlessly as it turned out, for the war-effort) were all re-instated. Some were not delighted, like the gay rights activists who felt that the tree-felling, shrub clearance and general admission of air and light into a usefully overgrown and discreetly scruffy patch was depriving gay men of a traditional nocturnal recreational space. But it seems to me that public spaces are for everyone and shouldn't be monopolised by one section of the community. I think that most people believe that the restoration has been a success and information boards show the original plans and maps of Repton's design. Russell Square is a large and welcome open space for adults and children (who love to run in

and out of the open fountain's wind-blown water jets on summer days) and in hot weather the grass is covered with prostrate office workers and students and residents from nearby flats. The tourists are delighted with the growing population of squirrels who now take daily photo-shoots in their stride but are, in terms of public health, about as desirable as the flea-ridden and ragged pigeons who also gather there. In the trees one sometimes sees blue tits and always plenty of blackbirds, scuffling in their rough and noisy way in the flowerbeds or singing loudly in the branches. Magpies also waddle around the Square. I spoke recently to an official of Camden Parks Department who told me that a pair of peregrine falcons had been spotted in Tavistock Square. In Bloomsbury Square tawny owls have been seen.

Today's characteristic Bloomsbury Georgian face dates from the epoch of Russell Square's construction. The demolition of Bedford House in 1800 marks a turning point as the Bedford Estate turned its mind to development and, as already noted, the open fields north of Great Russell Street finally succumbed to building. The Victorian writer Roland Dobie summed up what people felt in the second half of the nineteenth century when the new Bloomsbury building programme was completed:

> The admirable plan of Bloomsbury, as thus completed about 1850, subtly interweaving seven garden squares, with all its lines ensuring the widest distribution of sunshine, is not the creation of one mind, or even of one period.... But underlying it is a pattern far more ancient. The diversity in the sizes and shapes of the squares is largely due to that of immemorial fields and closes. The long thoroughfare near its northeast edge replaced a footpath in that quarter sanctioned in the fourteenth century. And the pleasant orientation follows the lines of one of the oldest thoroughfares in the London area, and of a green lane leading to a medieval manorhouse.[17]

Russell Square today has its fair share of pseudo-Georgian – like the university buildings on the Square's western side, and such genuine originals as remain are often actually facades with several houses knocked through laterally and linked internally, which means occasional non-functioning front doors and, no doubt, much internal modernisation. Originally, however, it would have had the perfect symmetry that remains now only in Bedford Square. These 'aristocratic' garden squares (which couldn't always be sold to aristocrats drawn more to Mayfair and points West) became the instrument of developing London's townscape from the eighteenth to the early nineteenth centuries. Most of London's building land was owned by the aristocracy rather than the Crown, and in this Bloomsbury was typical. In the eighteenth century Bloomsbury had four principal landowners: the Bedford Estate, the Foundling Estate owned by the Thomas Coram Foundation, the Skinner's Company Estate, and a private landowner, Edward Lucas.[18] In the early eighteenth century, as I've said, Bloomsbury was considered one of the healthiest areas of London and the presence of three houses of the nobility: Southampton (later Bedford) House, Montagu House and Thanet House meant that Bloomsbury Square was where the development started, as it was the most fashionable hub. The Duke of Bedford, who had done very well with speculative developments in Covent Garden, now joined forces with one of the most successful speculative developers of the nineteenth century, James Burton.

James Burton (1761-1837) began his career as a speculative builder in Southwark in 1785 but, in spite of having been trained as an architect, he actually designed very few of the buildings that became the signature of 'Georgian London' under his influence. He immediately saw the potential of the Bloomsbury acres and tried, unsuccessfully, to get the monopoly of developing the lands of the Foundling Hospital site but when that bid failed he nonetheless managed to build 586 houses there between 1792 and 1802, all the more remarkable given that this was at the height of the Napoleonic Wars and money was in short supply. The Duke of Bedford was impressed and hired him to develop Bloomsbury, Burton's drawing of the south side of Russell Square being exhibited in the Royal Academy in 1800. In his later career he played an important part in the creation of the Nash terraces around Regent's Park and in developing the Sussex coastal resort of St Leonards. Georgian buildings are generally spoken of with such reverence today it is easy to forget that they had their critics who accused Burton of being little more than a fashionable jerry-builder, turning out uniform brick and stucco terraces by the yard. He built 2366 houses in London between 1785 and 1823 so he certainly didn't lack energy.

In 1800 Burton began pulling down Bedford House and building two rows of houses on the south side of Russell Square pierced by what is now Bedford Place. He developed land belonging to all the key Bloomsbury landowners and built a villa for himself, with its own grounds, on the site that is now the British Medical Association headquarters in Tavistock Square. Sir John Summerson, author of the classic *Georgian London*, considered that Burton was "not a brilliant architect"[19] and singled out his Russell Institution which used to stand in Coram Street as a disaster that "combined Greek Doric columns and Roman arches in a peculiarly graceless fashion and was justifiably sat on by the critics." His actual method of building all those houses thought of today as typical of Bloomsbury was to sub-contract to smaller builders and much of the joinery and iron-work was prefabricated in factories such that, as Summerson puts it, "an individual Bloomsbury house would be a matter of assembly rather than design".

Not all contemporaries took this downbeat view of Burton. The nineteenth century Bloomsbury historian Roland Dobie claimed enthusiastically that

> a new and astonishing era commenced here in 1792, when an ingenious and enterprising architect, *James Burton esquire*, began to erect a number of houses on the Foundling Hospital Estate.... Let it be remembered that this vast speculation of Mr Burton's was begun and finished during a long disastrous war, most unfavourable to such an undertaking, yet he *sternly* persevered, and in spite of predictions to the contrary, succeeded and prospered to an extent far beyond his expectation.... The fields where robberies and murders had been committed, the scene of depravity and wickedness the most hideous for centuries, became, chiefly under his auspices, rapidly metamorphosed into splendid squares and spacious streets; receptacles of civil life and polished society.[20]

Inside a kind of stockade of iron railings within Russell Square gardens is a monumental statue of Francis Russell, fifth Duke of Bedford, Burton's patron. The Duke has his back to the rest of us, facing north the whole length of Bedford Place towards another statue, similarly placed in Bloomsbury Square, of the Whig politician, Charles James Fox. Both statues were made by Richard Westmacott and the idea was that these two Whiggish gents would contemplate

each other for eternity from their magnificent plinths high above *hoi polloi*. In 2006 I had an email from an old university friend, Chris Graham, then Director General of the Advertising Standards Authority but today the Information Commissioner, and always a devoted Liberal, summoning me to the laying of a wreath to mark the 200th anniversary of the death of Fox. I couldn't attend but I often walk down Bedford Place, a grandly attractive terrace, relatively free from traffic, and wonder how many people ever pause to look at these statuesque worthies from another era when 'great men' were honoured in bronze and stone. The anonymous author of *The Picture of London* (1815) explains its contemporary significance: "The statue is colossal, the attitude well-chosen, graceful and manly. His Grace reposes one arm on a plough, the left hand holds the gift of Ceres, conforming with the general plan of a monument intended to mark the Duke's fondness for agricultural pursuits."[21] Given that the Duke is famous for having turned ploughshares into hod-carriers in Bloomsbury this is slightly odd, but at Woburn he would have continued with the experimental agriculture for which he and his successors were known.

Russell Square's eastern side was largely demolished around the end of the nineteenth century to build hotels, some of which did not last and were extensively rebuilt in the twentieth century. One of the lost buildings was Baltimore House, built in 1763 by the seventh Lord Baltimore on the corner of Guilford Street and demolished to build the Imperial Hotel. If I stand on the spot today I can see a marble plaque set in the pavement with an arrow pointing to the Turkish Baths. This is all that remains of this facility though I suppose there's consolation in a Chinese medicine shop just nearby offering therapeutic massage. The Turkish Baths were part of the earlier hotel (I would guess where the new Imperial Hotel restaurant is now, almost at the north west corner of Queen Square where it touches Guilford Street) and themselves were on the site of a medieval conduit, sometimes known as the Chimney or Devil's Conduit,

supplying water to the area. A friend who used to live in Kentish Town tells me he kept finding barley growing in his garden, testimony to the agricultural past of the area, and likewise the ghostly history of water – conduits and wells, marshes and ponds, seems also to haunt Bloomsbury. In Russell Square, built on the Long Field or Southampton Fields of earlier centuries, where duck ponds proliferated, even moderate rain seems to result, quite quickly, in flooding of the park. We know all about London's buried rivers like the Fleet, away to the east of my patch, but all sorts of lesser watercourses are down there somewhere. Nearby Coram Street (formerly Great Coram Street) to the north east of the Square was once a sunken lane "bounded by stagnant waters".[22] Meanwhile that arrow, in melancholy fashion, leads absolutely nowhere.

Contemporaries always stressed the healthy nature of the Square and its access to views of Hampstead and Highgate to the north (which can still be seen from the upper floors of office buildings or hotels). It was always, as I have pointed out, very popular with lawyers and actors, and the portrait painter Sir Thomas Lawrence lived at No 65 (now under the Imperial Hotel) from 1805-1830 and built up a considerable art collection in his house. One of his commissions was the Cossack General Matvei Platov, completed in 1818, when his loyal Cossacks, mounted on small white horses, lowered their spears and stood solemnly on guard outside the painter's house while the sitting took place. Famous residents, like the diarist, Henry Crabb Robinson, the editor of *The Times*, John Walter, the legal reformer, Samuel Romilly, and Sir George Williams, founder of the YMCA (not to mention George Grossmith, co-author of *The Diary of a Nobody*) made Russell Square a fashionable location, but in the late twentieth and early twenty-first centuries offices and university buildings have largely displaced any residential population.

One cold winter night my wife and I went to the Annual General Meeting of the Friends of Russell Square, having for once remembered to renew our subscription. The meeting took place in the vestry of St George's Bloomsbury and the formal business was quickly despatched to make way for the real business of the evening: a jolly good old-fashioned feed provided by volunteers. There were lashings of sandwiches, chocolate biscuits, cake, and wine and a raffle with seemingly more prizes than punters, and 'a good time was had by all'. This excellent organisation runs a fund-raising bookstall under a canopy on odd summer days in the Square and organises coach trips to Woburn and other places, a reminder that, even in the heart of the capital, traditional local community life goes on as it does anywhere else in the country.

Sometimes, over the raucous sound of buses and cars and celebrating crowds, at dusk I can hear the gentle sound of an old-fashioned handbell ringing, as if I were in the playground of a school in rural Wales in 1900 listening to the schoolmistress calling her pupils back to their lessons. It is closing time in the gardens of Russell Square and the park-keeper is warning everyone that he is just about to lock up.

THE AMBIGUITIES OF MARCHMONT STREET

Is there such a thing as a 'typical' Bloomsbury Street? Probably not. Some would choose a terrace of Georgian houses, or perhaps one of the wide thoroughfares in the university or Museum district but today I am in Marchmont Street, looking up doubtfully at a fluttering banner, like something from a medieval pageant, carrying the logo of Camden Council: 'Love your local high street'. No one in Camden Town Hall seems to have read either *Brave New World* or *Nineteen Eighty-Four* and they clearly think it is their role to confront the local electorate with slogans that tell us where to distribute our affections. Like the fatuous 'Midtown' streamers which are trying to create a wholly factitious entity combining Bloomsbury, Holborn and St Giles into an estate agent's fantasy called 'Midtown', the 'love' campaign is yet another example of how 'cash-strapped local councils' find ways of wasting money on pieces of silliness. I have in my hand a copy of the latest *Camden New Journal*, a freesheet that contrives to be quite a decent local paper, which says that, to help the local high street businesses in the depths of a recession, Camden (the local landlord in Marchmont Street) is going to raise shop rents by 25%. The Gay's the Word independent bookshop in Marchmont Street may have to close. Perhaps this is what they mean by 'tough love'.

Actually I am fond of Marchmont Street, my local shopping street, in spite of its rather scruffy face. Named after one of the founding governors of the Foundling Hospital to the east, the Earl of Marchmont, it struck Virginia Woolf in the same way not long after she had come back to Bloomsbury to live in Tavistock Square. "Oh, the convenience of the place and the loveliness too," she wrote in her diary for 5th April 1924, "Why do I love it so much?"[23] In one of her letters she describes sauntering out to Marchmont Street to buy a kettle and some carnations – known to the locals as 'cars'. It's still where you go to buy stuff: cheap kettles, newspapers, buckets, binliners, paint-brushes, takeaway snacks. When Woolf shopped there in 1924 it was still a busy high street full of traditional shops. A marvellous illustrated book produced in 2008 by the Marchmont Street Association is packed with photographs that show how it once looked. There were butchers and bakers and fishmongers and fruiterers and cobblers and tailors, and a department store called Edwards which my friend Kay Birchley, who came to live nearby at the end of the 1960s, recalls had that old-fashioned system of brass chutes to send the money up to the cashier for each purchase. Even in the late 1960s there was no supermarket nearby and everyone shopped locally, but as any long-term resident will tell you, that ended when 'the Brunswick' was built at the end of the decade and a supermarket was installed. In the twelve years I have lived around the corner in Strachey Mansions a fishmonger has gone and, in 2009 the first Costa coffee chain shop opened. One only needs to go and take a look at Lamb's Conduit Street to see what the future will be: continuing gentrification and the replacement, inexorably, of traditional shops by chi-chi boutiques, wine bars, restaurants, and expensive niche businesses. If we really knew how to 'love our local high street' this area would be like the rue de Batignolles in Paris which has been, yes, 'gentrified', but where the shops sell delicious fresh bread, fruit, vegetables, cheese, charcuterie, wine. Why can't a decent baker flourish in central London, baking loaves with a bit of bite in place of those horrid supermarket versions pumped up with air and tasting like cotton wool? Continental Europeans, rich or poor, wouldn't stand for this. But at least Marchmont Street remains somewhere the less well-off Bloomsbury residents can stock up on basics that would be twice the price in Waitrose in the Brunswick.

The Bedford Estate had always been very restrictive about shops and pubs but consumer demand forced it in the early nineteenth century to zone certain streets like Marchmont Street for shopping. Even then they kept a very tight hand on the design of shopfronts, forcing potential shopkeepers to choose all their designs from a prescribed catalogue. Up to about 1840 it was a place where reasonably well-to-do people lived, like the watercolourists John Skinner Prout and William Henry Hunt, nicknamed 'Bird's nest Hunt' after his preference for that subject-matter for painting. That artistic connection continued in the twenieth century when the potter Michael Casson set up his first studio in 1952, in the basement of No 55. Writers have also been attracted to the street. Novelist and playwright David Storey lived in a second floor flat at No 45 from 1956 to 1961 and there wrote his first two novels, *This Sporting Life* and *Flight into Camden* and his first stage play *The Restoration of Arnold Middleton.*

The poet and critic William Empson, thrown out of Cambridge after a contraceptive was found in his rooms by college porters, fled to Marchmont Street in July 1929 and lived for two years at No 65 (now the New Bloomsbury Halal Bangladeshi butcher), finishing there one of the most renowned twentieth century works of literary criticism, *Seven Types of Ambiguity*, which was published in November 1930. On arrival he wrote to the critic I.A. Richards: "This is quite a nice room for 28/- a week, and I have a taste for squalor and cooking my own meals. I am trying to finish *Ambiguity* (it is over 60,000 words by now) and get it published, but I am much hampered by a doubt as to whether any of it is true."[24]

Deprived of his Fellowship at Magdalen, and his name scratched from the college records, the disgraced but precocious poet and critic set up in Marchmont Street as a freelance writer where he was cultivated by T.S. Eliot, Harold Monro of the renowned Poetry Bookshop and Sylvia Townsend Warner. He would eventually leave in August 1931 to take up the post of Professor of English at Tokyo University. He had a fair-sized room at No 65 in a house owned by Gilbert Back, a bohemian hospital consultant whose colourful wife Doris Russell later married the poet Edgell Rickword. A friend wrote of him: "He

is living in Bloomsbury in a large room, beautifully furnished above the waist-level, below a sea of books, bread, hair-brushes and dirty towels."[25] Empson busied himself applying for a reader's ticket at the British Museum and frequenting the Fitzrovia pubs, which were more lively and interesting from the Bohemian point of view than any Bloomsbury pubs have ever been. The Fitzroy Tavern, a favourite of Dylan Thomas, was the prince of these, presided over by Nina Hamnett, the legendary 'Queen of Bohemia'. Sylvia Townsend Warner gives a picture of Empson in his Marchmont lair in 1930: "I dined with W. Empson. I had gone a little frightened, fearing it might be a party of intellectual young things; but it was as though he had foreseen that I was a timid grandmother, for when I arrived it was to a very untidy room, with bottles and books on the floor, a delicious smell of frying, a saucepan of twopenny soup on a gas-ring and Mr Empson cavalier seul. So nothing could have been pleasanter. He had learned to cook because his sister runs Girl Guides." Another visitor was the poet Ronald Bottrall, who wrote a rather awful poem about it:

Hands always inky.
One entered skating on a kipper bone
And heavily collapsed on a commode
Garnished with scraps of egg and bacon.
Refreshed by tepid beer
Served in smeared tooth glasses
One settled down to hear
The youthful sage spinning his paradoxes.

Empson's story is interesting because it gives a little insight into early twentieth century literary life in Bloomsbury outside the charmed 'Bloomsbury Set' *literati* I shall be describing later. Empson frequently went to see Harold Monro at the relocated Poetry Bookshop premises at 38 Great Russell Street and caroused with other Fitzrovian poets. Strolling across Russell Square one day he bumped into T.S. Eliot on his way to the office at Faber and Faber and asked him about an opinion Eliot had expressed, in his preface to an anthology of poems by Ezra Pound, that a poet should be constantly writing, preferably at least one poem a week. In the centre of Russell Square, Eliot paused ruminatively and told Empson: "Taking the question in general, I should say, in the case of many poets, that the most important thing for them to do... is to write as little as possible."

The southern end of Marchmont Street was originally called Everett Street and in 1806 a linen draper's was opened there by James Poole who came to specialise as a military tailor before later moving to Savile Row and establishing that area as the centre of quality tailoring. Poole & Co still exists so Marchmont Street can perhaps claim the credit for having invented the brand 'Savile Row'. One of Marchmont Street's only two pubs, the Marquis Cornwallis (named after the former Governor General of India and Viceroy of Ireland at the end of the eighteenth century) opened in 1806 but the present building dates from the early twentieth century and was rumoured to have been frequented in the 1970s by the Kray brothers – not to mention Sandie Shaw, Jack Lemmon, and the cast in rehearsal of *Emergency Ward 10*. In the 1990s the pub went through some wobbly re-branding, briefly calling itself the Goose and Granite, then the Goose, before reverting to the name chiselled into its facade for all to see since 1911. It is now, like so many central London pubs, crowded and noisy and with much of its trade spilling out onto the pavement outside. It ought to be my local but I can't hear myself think or anyone else speak in there, so I give it a wide berth.

The pub was damaged in the Second World War in 1940 when Bloomsbury was rather a dangerous place to be with over a seventh of its buildings being destroyed and 426 people killed during the war. The nasty new post office building in Marchmont Street is built on the bombed site of a draper, a builder and bootmaker. Bloomsbury Building Supplies at No 39, where I get my paintbrushes and white spirit, has a memorial plaque to Charles Fort, the American founder of Forteanism "the study of anomalous phenomena", who lived above it from 1921 to 1928. London's 'blue plaques' are famous but there is considerable variety in these. Originally put up by the London County Council, and later the Greater London Council, they are now in the hands of English Heritage, a representative of which organisation I failed recently to persuade, as we munched canapés at the unveiling of a north London plaque to the poet Arthur Hugh Clough, to consider Sir William Empson for this honour. He lacks the necessary celebrity quality I was told. But blue plaques are now appearing in greater profusion, sponsored, for example, by the Marchmont Association. There are some that are brown rather than blue. Some, like that to Charles Fort, are freelance, and some older ones in Bloomsbury, like that to Henry Chadwick, in Montague Place, are heavy bronze reliefs, not always easy to read at a distance. But they are merely the tip of the iceberg. A recent addition in Marchmont Street was a blue plaque dedicated to the comedian and *Carry On* actor Kenneth Williams who lived over his father's hairdressing shop at No 57 from early childhood until 1956, aged 30. I imagine him raising his hat to William Empson or David Storey in the butcher's queue. ("Oooooh, William, I feel as though I've got all seven types of ambiguity this morning!") No 57 is still a hairdressing salon and another comedian, Catherine Tate, grew up above her parents' flowershop in the street, at the entrance to the Brunswick. Ricky Gervais lived recently in rather more style in a penthouse flat above Russell Square and Alexei Sayle lives near Lamb's Conduit Street, whose annual street festival he officially opened one year. I have spotted him whizzing past on a bike.

There is one other kind of plaque that the sharp-eyed will notice in Marchmont Street and elsewhere: the old cast-iron signs marking parish boundaries. These are usually late eighteenth or early nineteenth century and distinguish St George's Bloomsbury (SGB) from St Pancras (SPP), for example, or, in the case of the one on The Lamb public house in Lamb's Conduit Street, St Pancras from St Andrew's Holborn. The moral of this is to walk always with your eyes raised higher than ground level. When writing this book I have learned to look up because there is a whole extra dimension to the London street scene if you learn to look higher.

On the eastern side of Marchmont Street, where Edwards & Son Provision Merchants, with its brass money-chutes, stood until the late 1960s, there is now a large Alara Wholefoods store which, with Gay's the Word at No 66 and the recent arrival The School of Life at No 70, makes this side of the street begin to look like the 'alternative' side of Marchmont Street. The School of Life displays a weekly aphorism, poster-sized, in the window and I have a notion that Alain de Botton is somewhere behind all this, his name being given as one of the School's 'ambassadors'. His brand of easy to swallow philosophising seems to permeate the School's account of itself: "The School of Life is a new social enterprise offering good ideas for everyday living... we offer a variety of programmes and services concerned with how to live wisely and well. We address such questions as why work is often unfulfilling, why relationships can be so challenging, why it's ever harder to stay calm and what one could do to try to change the world for the better." It's hard to quarrel with any of this so good luck to them but I've got a sneaking feeling that it probably costs a bit more than an evening class over at the Mary Ward Centre.

In this same block is the revamped Marchmont Community Centre, which used to have excellent *Morning Star* book sales on Saturday mornings and hosted my residents' association meetings. Since the revamp and the installation of the usual paraphernalia of security buttons and doors it has a little less of a cosy 'walk-in' feel but it's still an important and vibrant centre for the local community, particularly the long-standing residents who provide a stable sense of continuity in an area that has seen many changes in the last few decades.

Marchmont Street carries on to the north across Tavistock Place and here the houses, built in 1807 by James Burton, as an extension of Burton Crescent, are a little more elaborate, or would have been if they had not been converted into shops like the Russell Supermarket over whose facade, a plaque tells me, the poet Shelley lived very briefly in 1815 and 1816. Burton Crescent I have already described under its new name of Cartwright Gardens (the name actually changed not principally to honour the radical Chartist but because a series of brutal murders there had blackened its name and the locals wanted to signal a fresh start). The Lord John Russell pub next door to the supermarket honours the sixth Duke of Bedford, who was twice Prime Minister in the mid-ninteenth century. Down the left-hand side is an interesting little alley called South Crescent Mews which looks as though it ought to lead somewhere but doesn't since it stopped being the stabling area of Burton Crescent.

Opposite is a well-known cafe, the Valtaro Snack Bar, with an apron terrace that is always packed, regardless of the weather, with people chomping their way through full English breakfasts – regardless of the time of day – and rather tempting plates of pasta. I pass these diners on my way into my dentist at No 98, whose premises used to be a fruiterer and grocer. At No 82 is Judd Books (named after the street to the east where the business began) which is an excellent source of quality remaindered books, run by two bookish gents with a nose for the sort of title I am always glad to pick up for a fraction of its cover price. It's good for literature, film, art and poetry and, in the basement, history and geography, travel, classics, philosophy and science. It's always a little bit disconcerting, however, when one sees a pile of one's own books out on the front table (they haven't actually been remaindered but the book trade has its mysteries and little caches of returned or 'lost' books sometimes surface and find their way into these places). Invisible from the street, behind Judd Books, is what is left of Marchmont Hall where the Mary Ward Settlement started life in 1891.

One of my favourite shops in this section of Marchmont Street is back on the Lord John Russell side. It is probably the smallest shop in Bloomsbury. Creative Gold opens late in the day when the proprietor, Clive Gilbert, arrives by motorbike and you get in by pressing a buzzer for the door to be released. But you can enter only if there is no other customer inside as it can cope with just one person at a time. Clive, a former scuba-diver, and Treasurer of the Marchmont Association which is active in promoting the street, told me recently that he

had just realised that his stock (on display in dusty glass cases on either side of the customer, who feels like someone trapped in a phone box) is increasing in value. He found that a pair of gold cufflinks was worth more for its current scrap value than it had been when he attached the original price ticket. The shop manages watch repairs, and sells second hand watches, jewellery, model soldiers, strings of pearls, badges, brooches, even a spiked German World War One helmet. Given his skull and crossbones braces it's no surprise to discover that his jewellery designs include what apparently is known as 'biker gothic'.

THE BRUNSWICK

Half way down Marchmont Street, on the eastern side, the older buildings suddenly stop and a radically different kind of architecture presents itself. In what still looks like a street of down-at-heel early and late nineteenth century buildings and cheap and cheerful local shops, a vast piece of mid-twentieth century radical architecture suddenly erupts and the whole visual landscape changes.

The Brunswick was a creation of the 1960s and has always aroused strong feelings. Brunswick Square, as an aerial view would show, was designed to balance Mecklenburgh Square to the east, the two squares flanking the Foundling Hospital in Coram's Fields. But a combination of neglect and bomb damage on the western side of Brunswick Square created opportunities for something new, a departure from the Georgian template. In the 1960s the conservation movement had less clout and bulldozers could sink their teeth with impunity into Georgian terraces which, as in the case of those by Burton, were cleared to make way for the Brunswick. These were in multiple occupation, and in such poor shape that they had actually been condemned by Camden Council as unfit for human habitation. A photograph of 1953 reproduced in Richard Tames' *Bloomsbury Past* (1993) confirms the dilapidated state of Brunswick Square.

In the centre of Brunswick Square today is a giant plane tree, *Platanus x Hispanica*, or The Brunswick Plane. Its massive girth is impressive but it has rivals such as the glorious horse-chestnut in full blossom on this April day. The plane is London's most famous tree but one also sees cherry trees, figs, horse chestnuts, lilac and dozens of other species in the course of the average stroll. The absence of London fogs means that sturdy battle-axes like the plane no longer

need to be the only tree that is planted on a wide scale. I do have a small problem with the plane that is to do with its pollen. At this time of year, springtime, it starts to shed pollen, and tiny little brown hairs that blow into drifts on the ground like snowdrifts. Fifty years an allergy-free zone, just recently I have started to succumb at this time of the year to a hard, dry cough that comes, mercifully, in short bouts when I am in the vicinity of planes. But, yes, London needs more trees.

At No 38 on the north side (adjacent to today's Foundling Museum) around 1911 Virginia Woolf shared a dangerously Bohemian four-storied house, where various genders and sexual preferences intermixed, with her brother Adrian, John Maynard Keynes, Duncan Grant, and Leonard Woolf (though not forgetting to bring with them Sophie, "a wonderful old family cook inherited from the nineteenth century"[26]). Unlike today's student shared houses, breakfast was provided "and every morning one notified in writing on a tablet in the hall whether one would be in for lunch and dinner. All meals were put on trays in the hall and one carried one's tray up to one's room and, having eaten, left it again in the hall," as Leonard Woolf later explained. If one was Virginia Woolf one did not wash up or peel spuds. They each paid £11 a month for this arrangement. Duncan Grant's painted decorations on the early nineteenth century wooden shutters of the house, of elongated, vaguely Matisse-like figures playing tennis, vanished when the house was demolished – tossed into a skip, used as firewood? All we have is a pale black and white photograph in the Tate Gallery archive.[27] Duncan Grant also painted 'On the Roof, 38 Brunswick Square' in 1912. Vanessa Bell later recalled of No 38 that "all sorts of parties at all hours of the day or night happened constantly. Rooms were decorated, people made to sit for their portraits, champagne was produced... to while away the morning sittings. All seemed a sizzle of excitement."[28] By the 1960s, however, Brunswick Square had ceased to sizzle.

The construction site was known in 1960 as The Foundling Estate and the prevailing planning wisdom was that the local area was dying and needed some sort of shot in the arm. In 1967 the Deputy Town Clerk of Camden announced: "It will bring back, into this central part of London, ordinary family life – in fact, it is what you might call a fist of family life thrust into this area of institutions, offices, hotels and student hostels."[29] The locals didn't always see it like this and there was a lot of debate in the pages of the *Evening Standard* and elsewhere, with many residents challenging the idea that there was no living community in existence.

The Foundling Hospital had been demolished in 1926 and the charitable foundation moved out to Redhill in Surrey, then to Berkhamsted. However, that arm of its work no longer exists with what remains of the Bloomsbury site occupied by the Thomas Coram Foundation, a more proactive children's charity. Planners saw the Brunswick as a chance to create a very 1960s 'megastructure', a new experiment in urban living. It was originally planned to extend as far north as Tavistock Place but the plan was trimmed. The architect, Patrick Hodgkinson, started work in 1959 to create this single, massive concrete structure, a pair of A-frames connected by raised decks and containing houses, shops and other facilities. The actual construction work did not start until 1968 and was finished in 1972. The five storeys of flats and maisonettes, with two subterranean storeys of car parking (how 1960s) was conceived as a private estate but when the developers ran out of money (partly because they found they had to pay compensation to the tenants of all those run-down Georgian houses that had to be demolished) the scheme was taken over by Camden Council, the beginning of a not entirely happy public-private partnership which resulted in some cuts to the original plans – such as the abandonment of an exciting-sounding glazed over winter gardens for the whole upper storey – though glazed over balconies remain on the individual flats. Today only 80 of the 400 flats are privately owned and some of the public tenants have been there since it opened in 1972, many now quite elderly but happy to stay on. The architectural guru Reyner Banham, in his 1976 book *Megastructure, Urban Futures of the Recent Past*, called the Brunswick "the most pondered, most learned, most acclaimed, most monumental, most bedevilled in its building history of all English megastructures – and seemingly the best liked by its inhabitants." That last assertion seems more or less true but nonetheless something seemed to go wrong in the 1990s and the central piazza between and below the residential blocks became a rather grim,

neglected space with the rather congested and scruffy Safeway supermarket one of the few seemingly viable businesses apart from the Renoir Cinema, a mecca for serious arthouse film buffs.

When I moved in to the area in 1998 plans were already afoot to tackle the moribund Brunswick but it was not until 2006 that the £25 million revamped Brunswick (whatever you do don't use the word Brunswick *Centre*) was unwrapped by the site's owners Allied London Properties, using the original architect, Patrick Hodgkinson who seemed to be distancing himself now in interviews from the 'megastructure' babble of the 1960s. Gone were the empty shops, the cheap Italian pizza place, the branch of Iceland (yes, mega-chic was not the dominant style) and that unappealing Safeway. In came a glittering Waitrose and a spread of glitzy (well, sort of) high street chain boutiques. It was a very twenty-first century shopping mall with no independent traders in the main area, only off-the-peg franchises, some of which, setting up in the middle of a recession, were poised on a knife edge. Some have gone bust while I have been writing this, to be boarded up with a lovely green sign that says hopefully: 'ANOTHER EXCITING NEW RETAILER OPENING SOON'. Not every retail space was let even from the launch of the new centre, and it's not surprising in current economic circumstances that some businesses have been unable to stand the pace. Plainly, it is more attractive than it was but it's too much like an airport shopping mall and desperately needs some independent shops and restaurants other than Strada and Starbucks and Giraffe. Couldn't the managers of the Brunswick offer favourable starter rents to a few mavericks to start up? An attempt has been made to introduce a regular farmer's market so that real bread and cheese can be seen fitfully. The crowds, mostly young, that fill the central space, browse the boutiques, and form unbelievably long queues for the Hare and Tortoise noodle bar (have these guys got a lot of time to waste or what?) seem to like it, but the poorer folk appear to have vacated the Brunswick as they have vacated the pricey Waitrose where the Saturday fathers, bambino strapped to their chests, wander up the aisles to choose their sun-dried tomatoes and look, in that terribly self-conscious Waitrose way, so *important.*

In 1975 Antonioni shot some of his movie *The Passenger* here with Jack Nicholson striding along the concrete walkways. The Brunswick is tamed now and it's hard to think that anyone would come here again looking to shoot an edgy, futuristic backdrop to an urban thriller. But the Renoir remains a gem, a laid-back art cinema that never gets full and whose unhurried bar staff are very soothing after a jangly day at the office.

Footnotes

1. Cited in Roland Dobie, *History of the United Parishes of St Giles in the Fields and St George Bloomsbury* (1834), p1
2. Cited by Gladys Scott Thomson, *The Russells in Bloomsbury 1669-1771* (1940), p26
3. Cited byE Beresford Chancellor, *The History of the Squares of London Topographical and Historical* (1907), p183
4. *A Survey of the Cities of London and Westminster and the Borough of Southwark containing the Original, Antiquity, Increase, present state and Government of those Cities written at first in the year 1698 by John Stow, Citizen and Native of London. Corrected, improved and very much enlarged in the year 1720 by John Strype, MA a native also of the said city* (1754) 6th ed
5. Gladys Scott Thomson, op.cit., p52
6. Strype, op.cit., p84
7. Cited by John Parton, *Some Account of the Hospital and Parish of St Giles in the Fields Middlesex* (1822) p371
8. *Letters of Thomas Gray* (1925) edited by John Beresford, p191
9. Gladys Scott Thomson, op.cit., p363
10. Cited by Eliza Jeffries Davis, in 'The University Site, Bloomsbury' reprinted from *London Topographical Record*, Vol. XVII (1936), p 74
11. Ibid., p68
12. Cited by John N Henderson, *A History of the Museum Tavern in Bloomsbury* (1989), p8
13. Cited by Clinch, p135
14. Cited by John Gatt-Rutter in *Italo Svevo* (1988) p195
15. Eliot, T. S. *The Letters of T. S. Eliot, Volume 1, 1898-192*, p. xvii.
16. See Peter Campbell, *London Review of Books*, Vol 28 No 23, 30 November 2006
17. Dobie, op.cit., p93

18. See Dana Arnold, *Rural Urbanism: London Landscapes in the Early Nineteenth Century* (2005)
19. John Summerson, *Georgian London* (1945), p154
20. Dobie, op.cit., p144
21. *The Picture of London* (1815), p160
22. Dobie, op.cit., p168
23. Cited in *The Story of Marchmont Street* (2008) edited by Ricci de Freitas, p30
24. *Selected Letters of William Empson*, (2006) p12
25. Cited by John Haffenden, *William Empson: Among the Mandarins* (2005), p261
26. Leonard Woolf, *Beginning Again: An Autobiography of the Years 1891-1918* (1964), p50
27. See Christopher Reed, *Bloomsbury Rooms* (2004), p7
28. Vanessa Bell, *Sketches in Pen and Ink* (1997) p109
29. Clare Melhuish, *The Life & Times of the Brunswick, Bloomsbury* (2006), p1

SOUTH

GREAT RUSSELL STREET

One of the hazards I face each day when stepping out into the streets around Russell Square is that I will invariably be stopped by a tourist and asked for directions to the British Museum, probably the most-visited and best-known building in Bloomsbury. Towards the end of 2009 the authorities hit on a brilliant idea that clearly had not occurred to anyone before: *they put up some signs* for pedestrians as part of the Mayor of London's 'Legible London' campaign to get us all walking. We have come a long way since the belief of 1960s planners in places like the Brunswick or the Barbican that the car could have a place in the modern city and today the pedestrian is back in favour (though not always so in the eyes of the aggressive urban cyclist). When I worked in the 1970s at the Greater London Council's Intelligence Unit, editing research reports (which was the sort of thing young graduates did when they couldn't quite think what else to do while waiting for the Great Novel to present itself) the Unit published a sensible short Research Memorandum called *Walking as a Mode of Transport.* The media got hold of it and had a great deal of fun deriding this alleged piece of pretentious silliness from the GLC. I can't remember but I'm pretty sure there were allusions to Monty Python and the Ministry of Silly Walks. It wouldn't be considered so funny now when, for all sorts of reasons and with personal health counting for as much as environmental considerations, walking is once again allowed to be A Good Thing. But of course one can't just put one foot in front of another. It has to be organised. Unlike cycling, where there are all sorts of funny trousers, brightly coloured helmets, gadgets and gizmos to be got, the city walker doesn't need very much to get started so the Mayor of London scratched his head and came up with *Information.* The Legible London campaign, with its distinctive bright yellow signs on panels carrying helpful maps, is a great innovation and I'm not

having a go. It is based on "extensive research" and the maps indicate areas that can be covered within a reasonable walking time and highlight key points of interest to help people find their way. So well done, Boris (as we call our Mayor, Boris Johnson, though never, I note, 'Blue Boris' like his predecessor 'Red Ken' Livingstone).

One might think that something as massive as the British Museum would be rather unmissable, but I am still stopped regularly in the street for directions. Today I have decided to approach it from the far eastern end of that street, on the north side where it hits Southampton Row, and where that little stretch of Georgian buildings known as Bloomsbury Place sits on part of the site of Southampton House, demolished in 1800, and now occupied by offices and several international colleges and universities. One of these runs a course on London in contemporary fiction and I was pleased to be invited in a couple of years ago to talk to the students about my 2003 novel, *Remembering Carmen*. This novel is set in contemporary Fitzrovia, west of the boundary of Tottenham Court Road that I laid down in order to demarcate Bloomsbury, so I can't say much about it here except that the students, all Americans, seemed to like the novel – or perhaps I should say, be stimulated by it. The central character, Carmen O'Hare, is a pushy, aggressive journalist and one of the students decided that she hated her so much that, with a pencil, she had stabbed out her eyes on the cover of her copy of my book. That's what I call incisive literary criticism. Unlike some book reviewers, these bright kids realised that you don't have to love the characters in fiction for them to work and we had a very lively discussion. They even suggested that I write a sequel (the book ends with Carmen going to New York and abandoning her lover). I really must get round to this. Soon.

Looking across the road I can see Bloomsbury Square, covering the space once occupied by the Earl of Southampton's "little town", which recently benefitted from Camden Council's splendid programme of historic square improvements. It's a far smaller space than Russell Square and it has an unusual feature in that it rises in a gently convex way at the centre and is surrounded on two of its sides by attractive town houses. Walking across its crown you feel in an odd way rather buoyant and superior. The information boards insist that tawny owls have been seen here but I can't claim to have spotted them. The square's north side fronts onto Vernon Place where it joins Bloomsbury Way, which in turn flows into New Oxford Street, all three streets between Southampton Row and Tottenham Court Road marking in succession the southern boundary of Bloomsbury.

Some of the houses in the south-west corner are quite early, dating back to 1744, and the early nineteenth century frontages are deceptive because they conceal in some cases seventeenth century interiors. At No 6 on that west side lived from 1817 to 1829 Isaac Disraeli, father of the Prime Minister Benjamin Disraeli. Appropriately, it is now the headquarters of the Board of Deputies of British Jews. In 1840 it became the first orthopaedic hospital in Britain, under the guidance of William Little, until this was relocated to become the Royal National Orthopaedic Hospital. This is the most appealing side of Bloomsbury Square and the height of the buildings gives it a special flavour.

Because Bloomsbury Square was always so fashionable, and was the first square to be built, it always attracted distinguished residents and many famous writers chose to live there – Charles Sedley the Restoration poet, Richard Steele, Mark Akenside, and Richard Baxter being a few of them – but in 1907 the author of *The History of the Squares of London, Topographical and Historical*, E. Beresford Chancellor, could write: "its day as a fashionable centre seems to have irrevocably gone."[1] Another hundred years later, no longer a residential square, flanked to the north by offices and university buildings, to the east by the backside of the former Liverpool Victoria Friendly Society building, and to the west by those attractive Georgian houses all in use as offices, it is visually pleasant enough but, apart from the office workers who come to eat their lunch in it, it is still not "a fashionable centre" as it was when Thackeray in *The History of Henry Esmond Esq* (1852) has Mrs Steele ask: "Do you know Bloomsbury Square...? Why, Bloomsbury is the very height of the mode.... 'Tis *rus in urbe*, you have gardens all the way to Hampstead, and palaces round about you, Southampton House and Montague House."

One of Bloomsbury Square's most important residents, when one thinks of the future development of Montagu House (aka The British Museum), was Sir Hans Sloane. Sloane, a physician, set up in 1689 at No 3 Bloomsbury Place and had a very successful and fashionable medical practice there, treating Queen Anne and Kings George I and II, among others. He was a pioneering doctor and became President of the College of Physicians in 1719 and succeeded Sir Isaac Newton as President of the Royal Society in 1727. He was a great collector of plants and specimens from his travels, coins and medals, and books, prints and manuscripts. He is said to have been outraged when Handel paid a call in Bloomsbury Square and put down a hot buttered muffin on one of his precious rare books. At his death in 1753 (aged 93) he bequeathed his entire collection to King George II for the nation, as the basis of the British Museum collection, in exchange for a grant of £20,000 to his heirs. On 7th June in the year of his death an Act of Parliament establishing the British Museum was passed but the Museum did not open its doors for another six years, in 1759.

Bloomsbury Square may have been fashionable, but it was not necessarily immune to the epidemic of street crime and burglary of the mid-eighteenth century which saw Sloane's house destroyed after burglars, who upon being discovered, lit a fire so they could pretend that they had entered the house in order to save it from burning. In 1751 the Countess of Albemarle's coach was held up in Great Russell Street by seven 'footpads' who robbed her and her companions of two watches and nine guineas. Horace Walpole said the crime had shocked all London. The proximity of the notorious 'rookeries' where crooks could quickly disappear, probably helped to make Bloomsbury Square a good place for criminals to operate. There were regular attacks on sedan chairs and coaches. The Square also saw its share of political protest. In 1765 hundreds of Spitalfields weavers attacked Bedford House, demolishing part of the wall on Great Russell Street, because the Duke was a harsh opponent of new customs duties on the imported silks which were threatening the weavers' livelihoods. Horse and foot soldiers were called out and the Riot Act read, but for four days and nights the weavers besieged the house before the troops finally dispersed them. Later in the century, in 1780, the Gordon Riots saw a particularly fierce eruption of drunken violence in Bloomsbury Square when the Lord Chief Justice, Lord Mansfield's house was burnt down. Dickens has a vivid account of this in *Barnaby Rudge*. The rioters also attacked Langdale's gin distillery towards Holborn and eight men drank themselves to death. During the week of riots, troopers were camped in tents on the fields behind Montagu House. But Alexander Pope, in his 'Second Epistle of the Second Book of Horace' stuck imperturbably to the 'fashionable' image of Bloomsbury Square, writing:

> In Palace Yard, at nine, you'll find me there;
> At ten, for certain, Sir, in Bloomsbury Square.

Leaving Bloomsbury Place and walking westwards towards the Museum, across the top of Bedford Place, nodding respectfully

towards Charles James Fox on his pedestal inside the railings of the square to the south, I get to the corner of Montague Street whose rather grand houses (if we close our minds to the bunks of the student hostel) are almost all hotels with gentlemen in bowler hats and long coats opening the taxi doors of very well-heeled foreign tourists. One day, coming back from the theatre, I turned into Montague Street and found myself walking along behind a quickly-trotting fox. He turned and looked at me disdainfully as if to say: "Who are you looking at?" then shot under one of the black wrought iron gates that protect the entrance to the gardens of the hotels on the eastern side of the Place. One of the most exciting art exhibitions in London of the past few years was the Royal Academy's Vilhelm Hammershøi exhibition, *The Poetry of Silence*, in 2008. The Danish artist painted a number of London scenes and his picture of Montague Street, looking north, shows a vista hardly changed since it was painted in 1906. The splendid white building with a long canopied wrought iron balcony on the corner is the new office of Faber and Faber.

THE BRITISH MUSEUM

Crossing Montague Street even the most bewildered tourist could see that this massive building rising up behind the black railings is the British Museum. The original seventeenth century Montagu House, "justly esteemed one of the most magnificent buildings in the metropolis"[2] according to the eighteenth century historian of London, John Noorthouck. And an earlier historian of London, John Strype, put it one of London's marvels: "for Stateliness of Building and curious Gardens, Montague-house hath the Pre-eminence, as indeed of all Houses within the Cities of London and Westminster, and the adjacent Parishes."[3] It was destroyed by fire in 1686. The house had been through colourful times, especially when the second Duke of Montagu's step-mother was in residence. She was quite mad

and thought she was the Empress of China. Guests sometimes played along with her fantasy. The house had been built in 1675-9 by Robert Hooke and was the grandest house in Bloomsbury, eclipsing even Southampton/ Bedford House. It was opened to the public in 1759 as the British Museum but, as the collection grew, rebuilding became a priority and Sir Robert Smirke was called in to rebuild in 1820, especially now that the library of George III had been acquired. Neo-Grecian was the architecture of the day and Hooke's mansion was swallowed up in the new design. In 1852 the Keeper of Printed Books, Antonio Panizzi (another resident of Bloomsbury Square), proposed a circular Reading Room to occupy the site of the central courtyard built by Smirke. The new architect of the Reading Room was Smirke's younger brother Sydney and the famous "round Reading Room" was completed in 1857. It was well patronised, with 182,000 people using it in 1887, for example, and its appearance was much admired in its Victorian heyday. Henry Wheatley's *London Past and Present* (1891) notes: "The colouring is of a light blue, the ribs and panels being picked out with gold, and the effect large, cheerful and luminous."[4] Another writer, George Clinch, wrote in 1890 that: "The internal arrangements of the Reading-room are perhaps as nearly perfect as it is possible for any reading-room to be.... The floor of the Reading-room is covered with kamptulicon [a Victorian invention of powdered cork and rubber] which deadens all foot-falls, and the tables and book-rests are so covered with leather as almost to prevent the possibility of disturbance; thus perfect silence is maintained, although more than three hundred literary men and women are working together in the same room."[5]

This was the place where Karl Marx famously read, and which was immortalised by George Gissing in *New Grub Street* (1891) which portrayed the lives of the literary hacks and drudges of the late Victorian book world. One day, Marian Yule is in the Reading Room, filled with that insinuating London fog that actually found its way *inside* buildings:

> The fog grew thicker; she looked up at the windows beneath the dome and saw that they were a dusky yellow. Then her eye discerned an official walking along the upper gallery, and in pursuance of her grotesque humour, her mocking misery, she likened him to a black, lost soul, doomed to wander in an eternity of vain research along endless shelves. Or, again, the readers who sat here at these radiating lines of desks, what were they but hapless flies caught in a huge web, its nucleus the great circle of the Catalogue?[6]

I have never forgotten my excitement at receiving my first reader's ticket in the 1980s and entering the Reading Room for the first time. You passed along a narrow corridor before bursting into the great circular space, like a footballer emerging into the glare of floodlights from the changing rooms at Wembley Stadium. At the centre was indeed the great spider of the Catalogue, heavy, leather-bound, printed volumes, alphabetically arranged, that one hauled out of their circular bookcases by the loop attached to the spine. I then wrote my requests on a printed slip of paper and delivered it to an official in the innermost circle. Later, a trundling trolley would approach one's station in one of the spokes of the web and the books would be deposited by someone in a blue overall. I was astonished at how *noisy* it was, from the crashing of piles of books onto trolleys, assuming that in libraries one could hear a pin drop in the reverential hush. But at least it was not as noisy as the new British Library where telephones, bleeping ticket-cancelling devices, conversations, laughter, all the fun and noise of the workplace happen actually inside the reading rooms, not like the austere reading room of the Beinecke Library at Yale where I once read, separated from the business area by a plate glass door, the notebooks of Matthew Arnold. If I had been given the job of briefing the architect, Sir Colin St. John Wilson, whose building I otherwise love (apologies to Prince Charles who thinks it resembles "an academy for secret policemen") and who I sometimes used to spot in the middle of the day strolling about pondering his creation, I would have told him to go and look at the Beinecke and try to separate the reading areas from the business areas. Each table in the old Reading Room was covered in soft green leather and one felt a sense of continuity with all the dead scholars who had mumbled and squinted at these dusty volumes over the past couple of centuries. In today's bright new, computerised, library at St Pancras there are only one or two dishevelled Grub Street irregulars, the majority of the readers being professional academics and postgraduate students, many of whom look as though they have just stepped off a Parisian *haute couture* catwalk.

In those days it was quite tough to acquire a reader's ticket. On 23rd July 1932 the British Museum grudgingly awarded a ticket for six months to a brilliant young academic, a teacher at Trinity College, Dublin, a past student of the Ecole Normale Supérieur in Paris, and author of a book on Proust (and thus, one might have thought a worthy candidate for entry) following representations from his publisher and a beseeching letter from himself. His name was Samuel Beckett.[7] Today it is very easy to get a ticket, even undergraduates with access to good college libraries and the University of London Senate House Library, being admitted, with consequent overcrowding and the erection of signs at certain times of year saying that the reading room is full. And in the public areas of the British Library, hundreds of laptop users, not a book in sight, spend their days, giving the place an admittedly bustling, lively atmosphere.

Back in Great Russell Street the Reading Room is now a museum piece at the centre of the stunning Great Court, designed by Norman Foster at a cost of £100 million in 2000 after the Library moved to its new site in 1997. At the centre of this high dome of light one can look around the old Reading Room and get a sense of it, mummified in heritage fashion, the unborrowable works of leading authors filling the shelves. In 2003 I met here Matthew Huxley, son of Aldous Huxley, whose life I had just written and he agreed to a snap standing in front of a section of his father's works. He died two years later and I am glad to have the picture and to have received his help and encouragement with the biography I had written of his father.

The opening of the new British Library was marked by a ceremony in which a group of writers and scholars was led formally through the virginal swing doors of the main reading room, known as 'Humanities One', to listen to speeches. I was one of this privileged group because, at the time, I was on a six-month Fellowship at the Library's Centre for the Book (a project which subsequently failed to thrive and is no more) and I found myself standing next to someone who seemed as bored as I was with the formal speeches. We exchanged a wry glance of complicity. His name was Harold Pinter. The book I was writing at the time was a biography of the seventeenth century poet, Andrew Marvell, who died in a house more or less on the site of the current British Museum Director's lodging, at the western end of Great Russell Street. No one (including his biographer) is absolutely certain what happened but it seems that the medical treatment he received for an 'ague' was rather heavy-handed, involving sweating and bleeding the patient, who, after these exertions, died on Friday 16th August 1678 in a coma. Marvell had taken out a lease on the Great Russell Street property in this rapidly developing part of London, in the name of the woman who may or may not have been his wife, Mary Palmer, to help a pair of dodgy bankers on the run from their creditors in Hull and was, as so often, living incognito and at the edge of things. His memorial is in St Giles-in-the-Fields church just outside my Bloomsbury boundary.

Today the British Museum, with its imposing Neo-Grecian facade in front of which tourists photograph themselves, endlessly, constantly throngs with crowds and, as when it opened in 1759, the collections of Egyptian and ancient Greek material are its showpieces. Most famous of all are the Elgin Marbles or, as we should say, the Parthenon marbles. I like the way the Greeks have built a museum in Athens ready to receive them but the very English response to the idea that they may be returned is: we think, not at all, sir. No chink has ever appeared in the armour of the British classicist (BM version). The Museum itself states officially that the sculptures, inscriptions and miscellaneous architectural features that form the collection were 'acquired' by Lord Elgin during his time as ambassador to the Ottoman court of the Sultan in Istanbul. They were obtained in Athens between 1801 and 1805 and later, in 1816, Lord Elgin sold them to the Government which then donated them to the British Museum. In 1832 the Elgin Room was designed to display them and now they are in the Duveen Gallery. I confess that I have always been disappointed with the famous marbles, which are all damaged and in pretty rough, incomplete condition as well as pining for their original home around the Parthenon, the central building of classical Greece. I much prefer, in a neighbouring gallery, the Assyrian bas-reliefs which are far more vivid and interesting. I see that Byron agrees with me, calling them "misshapen monuments" and writing in his poem 'Childe Harold's Pilgrimage':

Dull is the eye that will not weep to see
Thy walls defaced, thy mouldering shrines removed
By British hands, which it had best behoved
To guard those relics ne'er to be restored.
Curst be the hour when from their isle they roved,
And once again thy hapless bosom gored,
And snatch'd thy shrinking gods to northern climes abhorred!

Controversy has always dogged the Marbles, especially in regard to their treatment by the British Museum over the years. Quite apart from the damage from London's nineteenth century pollution ("northern climes abhorred") there were some disastrous attempts in the 1930s to clean the fifth century BC pentelic marble with scrapers and various solutions. The BM mandarins reply that Athens itself is a polluted city and they might have fared no better there. The debate remains polarised between an idea that there is a special iconic quality to the Parthenon marbles necessitating their restoration to their original setting in Greece and the belief that London does these things better, displaying them in a context where they may be appreciated globally (with the invisible rider, one always feels, that Athens is some sort of provincial outpost inhabited by excitable foreigners like the actress and former culture minister Melina Mercouri, one of the more impassioned and memorable advocates of restitution).

The other jewel in the British Museum crown, in my view, is the Department of Prints and Drawings, which regularly draws out of its store rooms for free exhibition a range of outstanding prints and drawings. I always suggest to anyone visiting London only for a few hours that it is invariably worth checking out the latest exhibition. Opening hours and access are today a little easier than they were in 1811 when, according to a guidebook called *The AMBULATOR or A POCKET COMPANION for the Tour of LONDON AND ITS ENVIRONS:* "Persons who wish to see the Museum will apply on one of those days [i.e. the open days of 10-4 on Monday, Wednesday and Friday] in the anti-room of the house, between the hours of ten and two, where they will be required to inscribe their names and places of abode, in a book kept for that purpose; upon which they will be shown into the apartments as soon as the first rooms are sufficiently cleared for their admission. No children under ten years of age, or persons who are not decent in their appearance, will be admitted."[8]

MUSEUM STREET: SEAMUS AND THE SHAMANS

Outside the gates of the Museum the hot-dog sellers continue their implacable trade and the shops sell 'I love London' mugs, miniature plastic red phone boxes, fluffy toy beefeaters, silly bowler hats decorated with the union jack, and plastic policeman's helmets. Tourism is one of Bloomsbury's principal industries and outside the Museum it reaches its gaudy apogee. It is time for a drink.

The Museum Tavern – which like so much else south of the Museum could have been swept away had the decision to move the library to a new site at St Pancras not displaced the original plan to put it here – is on the corner of Great Russell Street and Museum Street, opposite the Museum gates. Entering it for the first time in the 1970s, a provincial innocent, I was mildly shocked to see two fat red-faced gentleman at the bar kissing each other, although today it is not in any sense a gay pub. Originally known as the Dog and Duck, because of the popularity of duck-shooting at the ponds of the Long Fields to the north of Great Russell Street, this is one of the oldest taverns in Bloomsbury.[9] It was first started up in 1723 by John Smith and it was not until 1762 that it changed its name to the British Museum Tavern, fronting what in the sixteenth century had been a green lane in a landscape of rose fields, orchards, herb gardens, and large fields, overlooking the Licours Garden, but which was now Great Russell Street. The Bedford Estate ban on taverns and alehouses in Bloomsbury was lifted in the early eighteenth century and many now flourished. The Dog and Duck would have catered to the sportsmen by providing food and ale but all its former rivals, the King's Head, the Crown Coffee House, the Bedford Arms, the Duke's Head, have vanished from Museum Street (then known as Queen Street) with only The Plough remaining. Round the corner in Little Russell Street there were three more taverns, the Spread Eagle, the Pied Bull and the Mitre. I

draw consolation from the fact that there is a wine bar in Pied Bull Yard still, adjacent to the rear entrance of the London Review Bookshop.

In 1798 the British Museum Tavern was rebuilt, at a time when the Estate was once again trying to limit the spread of pubs, and in 1855 William Finch Hill, architect of many famous London theatres and music halls, was called in to design most of the buildings on the Great Russell Street frontage in what was known as "modified French Renaissance style". The pub was now just called the Museum Tavern. In 1889 the landlord, George Blizzard, a Worcester man whose father had taken over as landlord in 1858, commissioned architects Wylson and Long to redesign the interior. Known for their work in pubs and music halls, they tried to harmonise with Finch Hill's classicism and restraint in an over-the-top era and the result was today's 1890s splendour so much appreciated by tourists. The major feature is a long mahogany backfitting which dominates the main bar area (which in those days would have been broken up into smaller saloons). Just one of the original gilded and embossed mirrors remains in the backfitting, advertising Watney's Imperial Stout. It was the work of local glass manufacturers Samuel Trenner and Son. The Museum Tavern is considered to be the model of the Alpha Inn in Conan Doyle's 'Case of the Blue Carbuncle' and it is possible that Windigate, the ruddy-faced landlord in that story, could have been George Blizzard, landlord of the Museum Tavern at the time.[10]

By this time the British Museum across the street was becoming a good source of trade (in 1855 a meeting had taken place in the Tavern to campaign for daily opening of the Museum for the benefit of "the middle and operative classes") with those Gissing-like shabby scholars in the Reading Room coming in for a pint of ale and bread and cheese. But today the duck-shooters, the artisans, and the professional classes have gone and Great Russell Street and Museum Street are home to publishers, booksellers and tourist shops. The Plough, always popular with the Museum staff, and its upper room hosting occasional poetry readings, is the Museum Tavern's only other immediate rival. It is halfway down Museum Street opposite what is now a typical Bloomsbury shop selling Scottish tweeds to tourists but which, until 2007, was the premises of Peter Jolliffe's Ulysses Bookshop at No 40. Peter Jolliffe was a poet and bookseller specialising in modern first editions. I once was surprised to be able to buy from him quite cheaply what looked like a first edition of Bruce Chatwin's *In Patagonia*, but he pointed out to me that it was a 1978

reprint. I have it still with his thickly pencilled price of £5 on the flyleaf. Originally published by Jonathan Cape in 1977 at £7.50, a first edition of *In Patagonia* could command, in the 1980s, serious money. Jolliffe was a great friend of poets and Seamus Heaney was a regular visitor to the shop. He built up collections of Heaney and Derek Mahon and Edward Thomas and R.S. Thomas. Ulysses, the novelist Jeannette Winterson once claimed, was her favourite shop but Ulysses was also Jolliffe and the business died with him. Walking past I always look up to see the bronze sign hanging at first floor level, indicating that this was once the premises of the publisher George Allen & Unwin, and said to have been designed by John Ruskin, which is why it is known as Ruskin House.

Over on the western side again, print-sellers Abbott & Holder, whose shop at No 30 rises on several floors, with five gallery rooms, specialises in English watercolours, drawings, prints and oil paintings from the last 250 years. Founded in 1936 during the great depression by Robert Abbott and Eric Holder, the business has always claimed to be founded on the principle, as they put it, "that beautiful and interesting pictures should be able to be bought from income". For over seventy years, they say, it has been their policy to stock pictures that are "within the means of as broad a section of the population as possible". That must be why my wife and I have a lovely watercolour by Herbert Davis Richter (1874-1955) of a Mediterranean harbour scene on our wall at Strachey Mansions and the bailiffs are not knocking. Although most of the shop's stock is priced between £100 and £5000 they keep a £50 and under box which they say is a direct descendant of the five shilling box of the 1950s. I never fail to stop and look in their window when I am passing and try to ignore the rumours that the shop, like so many of its kind in this area, is vulnerable. Planners, retail developers and estate agents are not kind to small independent businesses like this, preferring big developments with deep high-street chain pockets.

Another famous independent in Museum Street, at 49a, is the

Atlantis Bookshop, the oldest occult bookshop in London, founded in 1922 and with the words 'magic' and 'occult' engraved in the glass above the main shop window, so if you are a magus, pagan, shaman or witch, get along there. In his massive 'biography' of London, Peter Ackroyd argues that the area of St Giles, which almost borders the end of Museum Street, with its history of quack doctors and alchemists, means that "the neighbourhood has never lost its oblique reputation for occultism and strange practice".[11] He points out that the Freemasons, the Swedenborg Society, the Theosophical Society and the Order of the Golden Dawn have all established themselves in the same parish of St Giles, from which Bloomsbury was partly formed by binary fission. He believes that Atlantis Bookshop, "which remains the most celebrated depository of occult literature in England", could be another example of a kind of *genius loci* which keeps like activities and people together. It's an interesting speculation but, taking Bloomsbury as a whole, you could also argue that there is an alternative rationalist, free-thinking, progressive and reforming, light-of-day tradition that is even more powerful.

Museum Street ends at my southern boundary, where Bloomsbury Way is just about to mutate into New Oxford Street. On the western corner was once the famous Mudie's Circulating Library, which played such a decisive part in Victorian public education. Founded in 1840, Charles Edward Mudie's library charged readers one guinea a year to borrow books and his powerful patronage partly accounts for the growth of the famous Victorian three-volume novel. He had a puritanical streak, banning certain novels of George Moore, for example, but he contributed to the success of Charles Darwin's *On the Origin of Species* by pre-ordering five hundred copies when it was published in 1859. The business was successful throughout the nineteenth century but eventually the rise of free public lending libraries saw him off.

BURY PLACE AND THE LONDON REVIEW OF BOOKS

If Bloomsbury's reputation is still one of literary and intellectual life then the London Review Bookshop in Bury Place, another of those streets running south from Great Russell Street in front of the British Museum, parallel to Museum Street, must be one its nerve centres. Today I have called in to chat to the bookshop's manager, Andrew Stilwell, and we park ourselves in a corner of the basement poetry section. Linked to the *London Review of Books* whose offices are just around the corner in Little Russell Street, the narrow thoroughfare that links Bury Place to Museum Street, the shop opened in the spring of 2003 and aimed to be, what it palpably is, a real bookshop for serious readers. No paid-for window displays, no three-for-twos, no hype or marketing nonsense, it is the sort of bookshop Parisians, for example, would take for granted, but which is increasingly rare in Britain. The window display actually makes you stop and look. These might, you think, actually be the best and most important new books of the month rather than some rubbish which the publisher has had to bribe the bookshop to exhibit. Inside everything is clean and new and stylish and there really does seem to be at least one copy of everything. They even have, *mirabile dictu*, a copy of my novel *Remembering Carmen*!

A couple of years ago they decided to open a coffee shop next door which has become a centre of bookish gossip although Stilwell wryly recalls saying to publisher Nicholas Spice back in 2003 when the bookshop opened: "We're here to sell books not coffee." This was an allusion to the then practice of chains like Borders. But when the shop called Afrobilia next door went bust they saw the opportunity to expand. It had been empty for two years and it gradually gave them the idea of the coffee shop, reached by a passage running directly from the shop floor. It is frequented by publishers like Christopher

McLehose, agents like Peter Strauss, staff from Faber and Faber's offices a few yards away, the *LRB*'s own contributing editor, Andrew O'Hagan, and many local writers – "Like yourself," says Stilwell courteously. There is a certain amount of trade from country and overseas *LRB* subscribers, making the pilgrimage, and sometimes tourists drift in asking to be directed to Virginia Woolf's house or some other Bloomsbury shrine.

"You must be mad to open an independent bookshop," everyone told them, but the LRB has powerful private backing and they have survived. They run interesting author events and an annual World Literature Weekend all of which brings in trade. But is Bloomsbury still a literary parish? Like me, Stilwell is gently sceptical. There is the BM, there is London University, but actually there are probably no more bookish people in Bloomsbury than anywhere else. He worked previously as a bookseller in Cheltenham and lives in a flat just around the corner and sometimes feels that he lives and works in a pleasant bubble "bordered by ghastly things". I know the feeling and share his view that Tottenham Court Road is perhaps "the most repulsive street in London". We daren't even mention Oxford Street. By contrast, Bury Place is a good place to fetch up, with its sober mansion flats, Museum Chambers and Russell Chambers, one of which bears a blue plaque saying that Bertrand Russell lived there, and its preserved Victorian lamp-post outside the dental surgeon's premises. At night there is little traffic and it has a surprisingly quiet neighbourhood feel at the heart of the capital, with boisterous all-night Soho not that far away.

Whether one would go quite so far as the late Victorian poet, John Davidson, is another matter. Famous probably only for his satirical ballad 'Thirty Bob a Week', Davidson published in the *Pall Mall Magazine* in 1906 a poem called 'Laburnum and Lilac', celebrating Bloomsbury and its garden squares:

> What? Russell Square!
> There's lilac there!
> And Torrington
> And Woburn Square
> Intrepid don

The season's wear.
In Gordon Square and Euston Square –
There's lilac, there's laburnum there!
In green and gold and lavender.
Queen Square and Bedford Square,
All Bloomsbury and all Soho
With every sunbeam gayer grow,
Greener grow and gayer.

I wonder if I could interest my publisher in a new project: *The Anthology of Bad Bloomsbury Verse*. There's plenty of material, as I have already demonstrated, and there's a bit more to come. On the other hand Christopher Reid's recent *The Song of Lunch* (2009) begins in Bloomsbury as his protagonist leaves a Bloomsbury publisher's office which it is hard not to think of as being the old Faber offices in Queen Square and observes that Bloomsbury is "a district of literary ghosts/that walk in broad daylight" before wittily summoning up some of those famous ghosts. Louis MacNeice's 1962 poem 'October in Bloomsbury' also conjures up some of those same shades and, like Reid, saves the reputation of poets in Bloomsbury with a fine short poem that concludes with Charles James Fox – who, "unconcerned in a bath towel sits on his arse in Bloomsbury Square/While plane tree leaves flop gently down and lodge in his sculptured hair".Walking between the tall, sunless sides of Little Russell Street (past the offices of the *LRB*) there is little sign of Davidson's floral gaiety though this area between Bury Place and Coptic Street was once the Licours Garden where medicinal herbs were gathered and Bury Place itself was a track leading to the Long Fields of Bloomsbury. In the middle of this bucolic scene, in 1716 work began on Bloomsbury's best-known church, St George's.

ST GEORGE'S BLOOMSBURY

St George's was one of fifty churches planned by the Fifty New Churches Act of 1711 to remedy the shortage of London churches (only twelve in the event were built) and it has always been controversial, especially its curious steeple surmounted by a statue of King George I, paid for by an affluent local brewer, William Hucks. The church was built on a rather constricted site squeezed between Little Russell Street and Bloomsbury Way and in spite of being one of

Nicholas Hawksmoor's most ambitious designs it had to struggle with the limitations of its position, long from north to south and narrow from east to west which has resulted over the years in some internal re-arrangement to accommodate more worshippers. The galleries (one for the Duke of Bedford and another for Lord Montagu) reminded parishioners of the rules of temporal power.

St George's has always stirred strong feelings. Horace Walpole called it "a masterpiece of absurdity", yet John Summerson in *Georgian London* says it has "the finest portico in London". George Clinch, the nineteenth century historian, opined: "With so much tuition, under a teacher of such good taste and eminence, one cannot help marvelling that Hawksmoor should have committed so grave an architectural error as the designing of the ridiculous steeple of St George's Church, which is awkward, unsightly, and wholly out of character with the body of the church, and in every way an objectionable feature."[12] A London guide of 1876 said it "enjoyed the privilege of being the most pretentious and ugliest edifice in the metropolis". This being Bloomsbury, with its tradition of not-exactly-brilliant topographical verse, an anonymous rhyme soon appeared:

> When Henry the Eighth left the Pope in the lurch
> The Protestants made him the Head of the Church;
> But George's good subjects, the Bloomsbury people,
> Instead of the Church made him Head of the Steeple.

Recently restored, it is surprising to discover that in the 1990s Hawksmoor's church was actually in such a state of decay as to be on a global list of threatened buildings. But with help from the World Monuments Fund and various other charities like the Paul Mellon Foundation and the Heritage Lottery Fund it was saved and re-opened in 2006 after a five-year restoration. Once the University Church (from 1956-1968) it was where the funeral took place of the suffragette Emily Davidson who threw herself under the King's horse at the Derby in 1913.

The controversial tower is in the form of a small temple with a spire on top forming a pedestal for the brewer's statue of King George in the costume of St George. The Fifty Churches Commission, who gave the project to Hawksmoor over an alternative design from Vanbrugh, rapped Hawksmoor's knuckles over this conceit but in the end he got away with it. In 1871 the lions and unicorns embracing the crown at the base of the spire, royal symbols,

were removed on public safety grounds and replaced with stone drapery. When the spire was restored in 2008 the lions and unicorns were put back again. Hawksmoor got his inspiration for the steeple from Pliny's description of the tomb of Mausoleus at Halicarnassus in Turkey which was surmounted by a chariot drawn by four horses. Outside, an impressive six-column Corinthian portico faces Bloomsbury Way (and the army recruiting office) and the church inside has many of the original mahogany fittings including the pulpit. The inlaid altar-piece was rescued from the chapel at Bedford House when it was demolished in 1800. It is a fine setting for Handel's *Messiah* and I have listened there to more modern music, the only way most of us get to sit inside a church these days. Ardente Opera's semi-staged dramatic 1941 Tristan and Isolde oratorio by Frank Martin, *Le vin herbé,* was one of the most remarkable concerts of 2010, on a bitter January night when the string section looked distinctly frozen in spite of the vigour and warmth of their playing.

As interesting as the architecture is the reason why St George's was built in the first place. The original parish church of Bloomsbury was St Giles, but to reach it the polite folk of Regency Bloomsbury had to cross the notorious 'rookeries', dens of squalor and vice that provided the setting for Hogarth's famous etching of 'Gin Lane' which shows the spire of St George's in the background. The new church would spare them this risky passage. Even as late as 1836 the rookeries were a major problem, as the Minutes of Evidence to a Select Committee on Metropolis Improvements confirm. A local resident, Mr T Waring, told the Committee that the district which straddled the two parishes of St Giles and St George's contained about 260 houses, many of which were "in the last stage of ruin and decay".[13] He said that houses were "huddled together in that part called the 'Holy Land', vulgarly called 'The Rookery'; in this small space there are 260 houses, each house averaging 20 inhabitants, or in the whole upwards of 5,000 individuals." In some houses there were fifteen inhabitants in one room, all lodgers: "The inhabitants live in the greatest state of filth, poverty and disease. I must tell you, that to these houses there is only perhaps one privy, and this privy is generally choked up and the soil is running over into the yard, and a great deal of the soil is taken out and passes out into the middle of the street every morning; there is no drainage there, and the water runs from street to street, till it comes to a street where there is a sewer." Waring pointed out the nature of the problem, a no-go area for policing in the heart of the capital of empire: "The district is in the very centre of London, and it borders on the principal streets leading from the east to the west end of the town, and it is the resort of thieves, prostitutes and others of the most depraved characters, and forms a safe retreat even from the present police." It was claimed that the very air of the rookeries was dangerous and infectious and that nine other adjacent parishes were affected.

The early nineteenth century historian John Parton, writing in 1822, before New Oxford Street was cut through the slums in the 1840s, considered that The Rookery went as far as Great Russell Street and: "are at present remarkable only for the general poverty and depravity of their inhabitants. The vast numbers of Irish on this spot, render it probable that this is the part of the parish where they first settled; certain it is, that it has been proverbially notorious for their residence for considerably more than a century. Dirt, and an appearance of extreme indigence, are the characteristics of the whole of this quarter. The streets narrow, and the houses for the most part old and ruinous, present, with the squalid looks of the inhabitants, a picture of wretchedness scarcely to be equalled in any other part of the metropolis."[14]

The solution was the usual one of urban planners: disperse the overcrowded poor and send them out to the suburbs in the hope that they will no longer be seen. But as Gillian Tindall, in her book about the Latin Quarter of Paris, *Footprints in Paris,* has shown, bulldozing the homes of the poor without giving them affordable alternative accommodation is not the humane and progressive act it might want to seem.[15] Mr Waring, however, was adamant: "By pulling down the aforesaid district, a great moral good will be achieved by compelling the above 5,000 wretched inhabitants to resort and disperse to various parts of the metropolis and its suburbs, where they would breathe in a purer air than by remaining and congregating in one huge filthy mass, in rooms where light scarcely enters and where the houses cannot be ventilated." The gradual loss of affordable accommodation in city centres (what remains in Bloomsbury is mostly centred on public and charitable trust housing in the eastern part) is a social change whose impact is still to be measured fully. Areas consisting only of business premises and a few mansion flats and penthouses for the well-off are truncated communities.

Parallel to Museum Street, running down from Great Russell Street towards New Oxford Street, is Coptic Street, and where it meets Streatham Street and the Wagamama Japanese restaurant chain has an outlet, stands one of the few remaining "model dwellings for the working classes" built on the former site of The Rookery and now being flogged off by the Peabody Trust. A few years ago, faced with ensuring that all their properties met the DHS or 'decent homes standard', Peabody, one of the pioneers in charitable housing provision, was forced to put around 1000 homes on the market in order to raise the £153 million needed to renovate its older properties. In the face of protests by tenants (and surely the voices of their own conscience) Peabody watched while the estate agents pounced, selling flats in the Streatham Street block, Parnell House, for £300,000. The letters chiselled on the facade: MODEL HOUSES FOR FAMILIES put there in 1849 when it was built by the Society for Improving the Condition of the Labouring Classes, one of the earliest and best architectural examples of its kind, now look rather ironic. It is the latest example of the phenomenon noted above where zealous 'reform' sometimes puts you where you didn't actually want to be.

Coptic Street was also the home of the Dairy Supply Company, when Bloomsbury's milk was supplied on the spot rather than being unloaded from supermarket trucks. This stylish 1888 building (once housing the studio of painter Howard Hodgkin) with the firm's livery still in place, including the DS logo on the wrought iron gates of the dairy yard (now leading to a trendy Pilates exercise centre), is an untypically characterful Pizza Express venue, the tiles and internal décor preserved. Actually I prefer the Greek restaurant opposite in Coptic Street, The Konaki, which serves reasonably priced traditional Greek food and, to the relief of sweltering Londoners in

summer, has an open air section at the back, though not quite as romantic as a harbourside at Mykonos. Rather, it's a piece of asphalt overlooked by the rear balconies of those model dwellings. On summer evenings, I have seen there the lugubrious film-maker Mike Leigh, sipping his retsina. Like our MP for Holborn and St Pancras (no mention of Bloomsbury!), Frank Dobson, Leigh lives locally in one of those solid mansion blocks.

At the end of Coptic Street the relative tranquillity of these little parallel streets running south from the British Museum, ends in the noisy traffic of New Oxford Street. Opposite is a very decent pub called the Crown, to the right of which is the striking brass and mahogany facade of James Smith and Son, manufacturers of umbrellas, walking canes and riding whips, unchanged for 140 years. On its eastern side used to be the restaurant owned by the father of the singer Cat Stevens (as he then was) who wrote his first songs there over the shop. James Smith and Son has been here since 1857 when the firm moved from its original 1830 premises in Foubert's Place. James Smith was a vigorous Victorian entrepreneur who founded six other businesses including a hatter's and a barber's shop. It was at the firm's rather more posh outlet in Savile Row that umbrellas were sold to people like Gladstone and Lord Curzon. James Smith established a reputation for quality workmanship and repairs and they specialised in making ceremonial umbrellas and maces and gentlemen's canes. There was a particular surge in demand for 'swagger sticks' during the First World War and the customer base is international, with one American client famously demanding a stick made out of every possible English wood. The package contained 70 sticks. Unlike working class housing and traditional dairies, the umbrella trade shows no sign of faltering and a lot of work has to be subcontracted to other small craft firms but Smith's has maintained its tradition of making umbrellas and walking sticks in the basement workshops at No 53 New Oxford Street, even if nylon is now the likely material of the covers.

Around the corner, just at

the junction with Shaftesbury Avenue, is the Bloomsbury Central Baptist Church. Built in 1848 it is something of a landmark in English nonconformity because prior to that date nonconformist and dissenting chapels tended to be tucked away out of sight and this occupies a prominent metropolitan position. It was flanked by the Bedford Chapel to the north (which no longer exists) and the French Protestant Chapel of the Savoy of 1845 (likewise gone). The building was financed by Samuel Morton Peto, who made his money out of the railway building boom, lived in Russell Square, and was a Baptist MP.[16] Back in Grape Street, an odd, sunless little triangle behind the Shaftesbury and the rear of James Smith, beer-drinking seems to be the religion and this paved space is often covered in outdoor drinkers hugging their pints in the summer months.

But already these streets have been touched by the contagion of Tottenham Court Road and Oxford Street a few yards away: crowds, tattiness, and a kind of anonymous tourist and tacky-shopping London streetscape that has very little idiosyncrasy or interest. I've had enough and turn back into Bloomsbury Street, past the Oxfam second hand bookshop, where I can never resist popping in for a browse, and then turn right back into Great Russell Street, walking along its southern side, rejoining the British Museum crowds. There are still a number of second hand book dealers here, like Jarndyce the antiquarian shop that specialises in nineteenth century literature. This was founded only in 1969, but the building dates back to the 1730s. A blue plaque tells that the nineteenth century illustrator Randolph Caldecott lived and worked at No 46 and it has been a bookshop for more than a hundred years. Caldecott used to illustrate his letters with drawings of himself at No 46 taking a glass of wine. Jarndyce has renovated the ground floor to give the shop the feel of a recreated nineteenth century bookshop with wooden panelling and floors and a working fireplace. The facades of this and neighbouring houses opposite the new British Museum were re-built around 1850 to make them fitting company for the grandeur of the building taking shape opposite, which meant that the stucco was applied but internally the original panelling and features were untouched. In the 1960s this whole area was blighted when it was thought that it was going to be laid waste for the building of the new British Library but after that plan was abandoned in 1974 confidence started to ebb back. There are several specialist booksellers in Great Russell Street, including Arthur Probsthain at No 41, one of the leading oriental and African booksellers in the world, established in 1903. As bibliophiles like me

keep saying, one always holds one's breath when entering second hand booksellers, fearful that the last blast of unwholesome air from soaring inner city rents or the shift to internet bookselling will finish them off. But, for now, they are still there.

A little further along, at the corner of Bloomsbury Square again, is a stuccoed building remodelled in 1777 by John Nash in his grand style as two houses, one of which he occupied. In 1860 the two were combined and occupied by the Royal Pharmaceutical Society, whose name is still on the facade though they moved out in 1976. Prior to this the building had been the headquarters of the Royal Literary Fund, now in premises off Fleet Street. The newest literary addition to Great Russell Street, mentioned above, is Faber and Faber who now occupy that atrractive building at No 77 on the corner of Great Russell Street and Montague Place, called Bloomsbury House. Faber, the last of the big independent publishers, has moved quite frequently over the years but always within Bloomsbury. I used to walk wistfully past its HQ in Queen Square wondering if the collection of poems I sent them in the early 1980s (with a stamped, addressed envelope) would ever emerge. Three decades on, I think I have decided that I should no longer hold my breath. Perhaps, during one of the moves, they were accidentally placed in the removers' crate marked: 'Rubbish'. ("Wots this, John?" "Nah, chuck it.")

This could turn out to be the correct verdict of posterity.

Notes

1. E. Beresford Chancellor, *The History of the Squares of London Topographical and Historical* (1907), p200

2. John Noorthouck, *A New History of London including Westminster and Southwark to which is added a general survey of the whole: describing the public buildings, late improvements, &c* (1773), p742

3. *A Survey of the Cities of London and Westminster and the Borough of Southwark containing the Original, Antiquity, Increase, present state and Government of those Cities written at first in the year 1698 by John Stow, Citizen and Native of London. Corrected, improved and very much enlarged in the*

year 1720 by John Strype, MA (1754) 6th ed, p84
4. Henry Wheatley, *London Past and Present* (1891) [revised edition of 1849 *Handbook of London* by Peter Cunningham], p271
5. George Clinch, *Bloomsbury and St Giles, Past and Present* (1890), p145
6. George Gissing, *New Grub Street* (1891) edited by G.W. Stonier, Oxford, 1958, p110, Chapter VIII
7. *TheLetters of Samuel Beckett 1929-1940* (2009), edited by Martha Dow Fehsenfeld and Lois More Overbeck, p109
8. *The AMBULATOR or A POCKET COMPANION for the Tour of LONDON AND ITS ENVIRONS* (11th edition, 1811) p24
9. I am much indebted here to John N. Henderson's excellent short history: *A History of the Museum Tavern in Bloomsbury* (1989)
10. See Henderson, p24
11. Peter Ackroyd, *London:The Biography* (2000), p140
12. Clinch, op. cit., p128
13. Minutes of Evidence Taken Before the Select Committee on Metropolis Improvements, 19 July 1836, *Hansard* p34
14. John Parton, *Some Account of the Hospital and Parish of St Giles in the Fields Middlesex* (1822), p153
15. Gillian Tindall, *Footprints in Paris: a few streets, a few lives* (2009), pp129ff
16. See Faith Bowers, *A Bold Experiment: The Story of Bloomsbury Chapel and Bloomsbury Central Baptist Church 1848-1999* (1999)

EAST

NEW PRINT, OLD PRINT: GRAY'S INN ROAD

Although there is ready agreement about the western, northern and southern boundaries of Bloomsbury its eastern boundary is more debatable. I have chosen to make Gray's Inn Road (formerly Gray's Inn Lane) the eastern march but some would go as far as cutting off Bloomsbury by a line running from north to south along Woburn Place and Southampton Row which I think excludes too much that is vital, even if, as I have already written, the far north eastern corner around King's Cross may seem to be stretching a point.

The south eastern corner of my Bloomsbury is where Gray's Inn Road meets Theobalds Road (or Theobald's Road to some, including the makers of the local council's street signs, who prefer to insert the apostrophe). The boundary post is the Yorkshire Grey pub (rumoured to have been used by the fugitive Lord Lucan). Not far along Gray's Inn Road are the headquarters of ITN, which reminds me that I have in the past seen the Channel 4 news reporters nibbling a sandwich at Pret à Manger on the opposite corner here. This end of Gray's Inn Road is rather nondescript, with the sort of shops that supply the predominant office trade of the area: restaurants, snack bars and wine bars, bicycle shops, bag-shops, print bureaux. At weekends Bloomsbury, like most city centre areas, changes its character and feel. Oxford Street and Leicester Square never sleep but in the City of London the change can be dramatic, with total silence descending on some streets, and many premises, including pubs and restaurants and cafés, closed until Monday morning. Central Bloomsbury is busy seven days (and nights) a week but here in Gray's Inn Road that melancholy weekend feel makes it even more desolate. Cities need permanent residents to keep them alive.

Almost immediately, as I step smartly into Gray's Inn Road, I spot Adana, the shop that print-hobbyists used to visit for their supplies in that far-off pre-digital era when a shop selling real metal type could make a living. Adana is still here at No 162 but these days it functions with more modern technology. It's where my agent, in one of the little streets off Gray's Inn Road, today sends hopeful manuscripts for copying, but when I first called in I had succumbed to the idea that once gripped Leonard and Virginia Woolf: of becoming my own printer in a very small way. Through *Exchange and Mart* I bought an Adana hand press, a great heavy iron thing that it was just about possible to lift. You set your own type – *each individual letter* – by hand (the metal type was sold at Adana in Gray's Inn Road until 1999) and packed it into a wooden frame, inked a circular metal platen then hauled on the handle to imprint copy onto paper. As the editor of Liverpool University student paper *Guild Gazette* in the 1970s I had watched the old-fashioned letterpress printers, Lyons, in a cavernous basement in Liverpool's London Road setting up type (which rattled off a linotype machine that looked a bit like a loom and at which the typesetter sat) and admired this dying craft. The Lyons boys would not have approved of my amateurish attempts, but, like the Woolfs who were rejected by the colleges of printing and had to teach themselves in order to launch the Hogarth Press, I had a go at printing poems on cards. I was influenced by John Fuller's Sycamore Press, that operated from his garage in Oxford, but I lacked either the patience or the skill (or do I mean both?) and my career as a printer died not long after it began. The cast iron hand press, which I had mangled to such an extent that it was probably unusable, went to the recycling depot less than a year ago. But I do still have a copy of the Sycamore Press *Confidential Chats with Boys* by Alan Hollinghurst, which is now worth several times more than I ever paid for my hand-press. And you can run off anything you like from your USB-stick at Adana's shop today. Progress.

Gray's Inn Road, frankly, doesn't improve very much as I move northwards. In 1986 Rupert Murdoch moved *The Times* from New Printing House Square in Gray's Inn Road to new premises at Wapping (another new printing technology story) by which time I myself was a journalist in Clerkenwell, just to the east, working on the first issues of a new magazine called *Social Services Insight*, which was at the cutting edge of this new typesetting revolution. We struggled to come to terms with these funny new things called word processors that had replaced our battered and food-impregnated manual typewriters. Apart from ITN, inside its plate-glass fortress (designed by Norman Foster out of the raw materials of the vacated *Times* offices), there

isn't much of a buzz along the street now. The spirits of Harold Evans and past legendary journos have evaporated. As I approach the northern end of Gray's Inn Road memory is stirred by the distant sight of the Lucas Arms, a pub opposite the National Union of Journalists' offices where I occasionally attended branch meetings.

THE LONDON WELSH

Just before that however, is Canolfan Cymry Llundain, the London Welsh Centre at No 157-163. Clearly I had better gatecrash this. I arrive on a Saturday morning at this rather old-fashioned building and there's no one around who looks in a position to give me permission to enter so I wander into the panelled foyer and peer at the noticeboards to see what's on. The London Welsh Centre Theatre Upstairs proudly presents an Old Time Music Hall ("fully costumed show with guest artistes") on the first Friday of each month. The Centre is also the base for the London Welsh Male Voice Choir, founded in 1902, and constantly busy with engagements at home and abroad. The choir's brochure asks a series of interesting questions: "When was the last time the hairs stood up on the back of your neck?" While you're waiting to answer that one they pop another: "Can you handle the passion?" I am not sure, actually, but here comes the next question: "How Fast Can Your Toes Tap?" This all sounds a bit of an emotional rollercoaster for me but at least the London Welsh are doing something to inject passion and energy into Gray's Inn Road. This is clearly a lively organisation, under the presidency of Huw Edwards the TV presenter, and there are plans for refurbishment of the Gray's Inn premises. Its poetry readings, comedy club and other activities make this an important outpost of Welsh culture at the perimeter of Bloomsbury.

Higher up at 261 the Clink Backpacker Hostel reminds me that there are several such cheap hostels in Bloomsbury, such as the YHA in Euston Road, the Generator off Tavistock Place and the Astor Hostel in Montague Street.

Given the sky-high cost of hotel rooms in central London this can only be a good thing for young travellers and backpackers. Watching a young couple emerge with a tottering backpack as high as Centre Point I wonder why it is that I always travel so light, surprising hoteliers and baggage handlers around the globe. Trying to escape the heavy burden of possessions and sheer *stuff* we all tote around, I suppose. The illusion of freedom and being unburdened, of treading lightly on the earth as Bruce Chatwin used to say.

DOUGHTY STREET

The petering out of Gray's Inn Road at its northern end into traffic and scruffiness makes me want to start my exploration of eastern Bloomsbury from scratch again so I turn tail and walk back to Theobalds Road. This time I start from a point a little further west, by turning into John Street, which soon becomes Doughty Street, parallel to Gray's Inn Road. I head north once more. This is much more promising. It is a wide, graceful street flanked on both sides by Georgian houses mostly occupied by barristers' chambers, including the formidable Doughty Street Chambers (at premises on *both* sides of the street) which houses such superstars of the progressive law as Geoffrey Robertson QC and Helena Kennedy QC. Until very recently the *Spectator* magazine was here, and most of those black-painted doorways set in white stucco facades lead into offices of organisations or corporations, though, as with most Bloomsbury streets and squares, there is some residential occupation.

Returning to my earlier theme of the 'typical' Bloomsbury street, perhaps John Street/Doughty Street is it? After all, there are the familiar stuccoed Georgian facades and intricate fanlights over each door. There is the sense that these houses were once lived in but are now largely business premises, and that behind those early nineteenth century facades the interiors will have been modernised and re-shaped to meet the needs of the twenty-first century office while at the same time presenting a comfortably 'heritage' face to the world.

So I take my walk down the western side of the street as far as Guilford Street then back up again on the eastern side, trying to take more than usually exact note of what is here. I note the miscellaneous premises, but first a heavy bronze plaque to Sir John Kirk (1847-1922) the nineteenth century Christian philanthropist and advocate of the ragged schools movement who was also dedicated to an organisation called The Pure Literature Society, which turns out to have more to do with the avoidance of 'unhealthy' books than with aesthetic disdain for vulgar social realism. There is a preponderance of publishing (*Loot* magazine, the International Publishing Group) and public relations agencies and, of course, barristers, since Gray's Inn is around the corner. At No 14 a brown London County Council plaque marks the residence of the celebrated wit Sydney Smith (1771-1845), who was co-founder of one of the most famous nineteenth century reviews, the *Edinburgh Review* and who campaigned for Catholic Emancipation and many other causes. The poet Charlotte Mew lived at No 10 and the film and drama critic, James Agate, at No 14 so the 'typical' literary flavour of Bloomsbury is being maintained.

After the British Thoracic Society I cross and come back on the eastern side, past something called The Creative Agency, then an association of French barristers, chartered accountants, a firm of "wealth management consultants" (not really relevant to me), the University of Delaware, the literary agents, Sheil Land, the Fulbright Commission in a very sleekly maintained property, a plaque to writers Vera Brittain and Winifred Holtby who lived at No 58 in the early twentieth century, a polite genuflection towards my own agent at A.P. Watt (London's oldest literary agency) on the corner of Roger Street (a street that once housed Dr Tibble's Chocolate Factory around 1900), then more institutions like the Chartered Institute of Water and Environmental Management, the Society for the Protection of Animals Abroad (with its 'I LOVE DONKEYS' stickers on the windows) and the registered office of the Free Painters and Sculptors, which turns out to be free as in freedom of expression, not as in help yourself from the box. Founded in 1952 and originally associated with the Institute for Contemporary Arts (ICA) these artists formed a group devoted to freedom of expression, a battle one might have thought was won by visual and plastic artists in the UK a long time ago. Solicitors Oury Clark at No 10 John Street, a firm specialising in human rights abroad, especially in relation to prisoners on death row, display a very large bracket clock over No 11 inscribed 'Royal Oak' the vestige of the mutual society of that name which was here until the early 1980s. Right at the end of the street is a rather more down to earth premises, OLCI, offering training courses to plumbers and electricians, a change from the barristers and accountants and patent attorneys.

But, for the visitor, Doughty Street means one thing in particular: Dickens House at No 48, housing the Dickens Museum. Dickens lived here from 1837 until 1839 and it is the only one of his various residences in London that is still standing. It's a slightly dusty, quirky sort of place and could do with some beefing up of its displays with better explanatory material but it's well worth visiting in order to see what a relatively unimproved nineteenth century Bloomsbury interior looks like over several floors. And you can buy a Sam Weller bone china thimble, an Oliver Twist horse brass or a Uriah Heep Toby jug as a memento.

Back in Theobalds Road the traffic is constant (cars, bendy buses, taxis) and I am tempted to cut in again and wander along Doughty Mews behind Doughty Street where cobblestones and tarted up former commercial premises create a quiet retreat from the urban noise. But I stay where I was, heading west again until, in front of Holborn Library I look across from the front library entrance to a building opposite (technically outside my patch) called Raymond Buildings. Here, in the flat of the Edwardian man of letters Edward Marsh, just before the First World War, Rupert Brooke spread himself out on the carpet and hammered out, with Marsh and others, the idea of the famous Georgian Poetry anthologies.

GREAT JAMES STREET AND RUGBY STREET

Another delve northwards into my third parallel street to Gray's Inn Road brings me to Great James Street. Pevsner quite rightly calls this little street "a gem". It contains some of Bloomsbury's loveliest Georgian houses, dating back to 1721, and those semi-circular fanlights or squarer 'segment-headed windows' over the wide doors carry a unique signature, each one slightly different from its neighbour (allegedly to help the illiterate postmen and delivery boys of another era identify the house they wanted) and often placed under a door-hood supported by carved brackets. At No 16, now the offices of the interesting sounding Brazilian Aeronautical Commission in Europe and next door to the Federation of Master Builders, was the 1920s headquarters of Francis and Vera Maynell and David Garnett's Nonesuch Press, which produced fine editions of the literary classics on delicate india or bible paper. The street bristles with literary associations even though there is only one blue plaque, to Dorothy L. Sayers, the detective story writer who lived here for 20 years from 1921 to

1941. In the 1840s George Meredith lived at No 26, E.V. Lucas at No 5 in the 1890s, and novelist and critic Frank Swinnerton at No 4. Leonard Woolf worked at No 38 in the 1920s when it was the offices of the influential magazine *The Nation*, later absorbed into the *New Statesman*. Gerald Brenan, author of the travel classic *South from Granada*, lived at No 14 from 1927 to 1929 after starting out nearby in Millman Street, and described Great James Street as quite simply "the most beautiful street in London". He lived in an attic flat at the top of No 14, less grand than the rooms on the lower floors, and later recalled his "eighteenth century fireplace full of mousetraps".

Once again I look up and down the street, speculating as to what the interiors are like. Today, thanks to Cardiff-born John Davies, managing partner at Pattinson & Brewer solicitors at No 30, I am invited inside to see for myself. He makes the obvious point that Georgian houses are not necessarily the best kind of design for modern office life but Pattinson & Brewer have carefully preserved the beautiful wooden banisters, some semi-circular oak doors, and a wonderful device used for summoning servants from the lower depths of the house. A little peg is taken out of a hollow wooden tube in the corner of John Davies' secretary's office and blown like a whistle, the sound travelling down the tube. Internal email has no doubt replaced it today but it is yet another reminder of how the Bloomsbury house expressed in its construction social hierarchies that must once have seemed permanent.

"I have always seen it as a village," says John Davies of his *petit quartier* of Great James Street, Rugby Street, and Lamb's Conduit Street where he has worked for 35 years. The firm used to get its milk delivered from Glyn and Margaret Davies, a Welsh-speaking couple in striped aprons, now retired, who ran a dairy called French's Dairy. Their parents founded the business but the premises is now a designer jewellery shop with several outlets operating under the French's Dairy label. That kind of transformation is very Bloomsbury: the old artisanal memory preserved in designer outlets

that no common or garden dairyman could afford to shop in. The roll call of deceased trades in and around Lamb's Conduit Street includes: chandlers, boot repairers, signwriters, patent medicine makers, and oil and colour men. There was a Greek Cypriot dry cleaners next door to French's and that premises is now a swanky interior designer called The English House which has done work for Prince Charles. John Davies recalls butchers, bakers, fishmongers, ordinary cafés, most of which have vanished. Following his direction along Great James Street and turning left at the Rugby Arms, a nice Shepherd Neame pub, into Rugby Street (whose name reminds one that Rugby School owns land here) where French's is located, I see, on the opposite side, No 18, where Ted Hughes rented an apartment in the late 1950s. On March 23, 1956, he spent his first night here with Sylvia Plath before she left for Paris the next day, an event commemorated by his poem '18 Rugby Street' in the collection *Birthday Letters*. The poem refers to the "Victorian torpor and squalor" of No 18, which was in multiple occupation and on each of the four floors the tenants bed-hopped in a "laboratory of amours". A Belgian girl in the ground floor flat entertained a second hand car dealer and stored his exhaust silencers and car parts. Hughes sat alone in his flat writing at an old joiner's bench that stood in as desk and table, and it was here that he and Plath spent their wedding night in the single bed.

Another occupant of No 18 in the 1950s was Jim Downer (whose later achievements were to include the invention of the Travelator). Hughes took over Downer's manuscript of a children's book and it disappeared, only to re-emerge in Hughes' papers after his death and be published in 2009 by Thames and Hudson as *Timmy the Tug*. In an afterword, Jim Downer described the days at No 18, the fact that there was no water to each flat, only cold water on the landings, an outside lavatory at the bottom, and the only bath one could get was at the public facilities at Holborn Baths. Ted and Sylvia were married in June 1956, a short walk away in the church of St George-the-

Martyr in Queen Square, an event also recorded in *Birthday Letters* in the poem 'A Pink Wool Knitted Dress'. It was at the height of austerity Britain with Hughes wearing his one utility suit and Sylvia's mother the only guest. They even had to rope in the sexton to be best man although he was trying to organise a group of children into a bus to take them to the zoo.

Next door, No 20, a tiny, narrow house, was the location of the Church of Humanity, catching the attention of Henry James in one of his travel essays. The Bloomsbury Church was founded by Richard Congreve, a former Anglican priest and disciple of the Positivist philosopher, Auguste Comte, who was the original founder of the Religion of Humanity. On 9th January 1910 – or "the 9th day of the month of Moses in the year 56 of the Positivist era" to the disciples of the Church of Humanity – Philip Thomas delivered a sermon celebrating "this first Temple of Humanity in Britain" in which he explained that, after some time as a lecturer to various ethical societies, he had discovered the works of Comte and the experience had been "a glorious revelation".[1] He told the faithful: "This Church has never yet drawn the multitude; but it exists under the auspices of mighty spiritual genius; it has been the meeting-place and field of labour of many elect souls." This seems to hint that larger premises would not, after all, be needed. He explained that it was part of a movement "towards making religion more human, more earth-centred – directed more towards ennobling this present life", the implication being that conventional Christianity was too pre-occupied with the life to come. Thomas described Richard Congreve, as "the St. Augustine of Positivism who planted the Cause in England and became the first pioneer of the Religion of Humanity". The sermon concluded with a special prayer addressed to "our Virgin Mother, Humanity". This curious pseudo-religion, with feast days for various secular saints like Socrates and Shelley, whose busts were ranged around the 'church', survived until the early 1930s when the premises were closed – but they soon re-opened as a dance-hall.

Rugby Street was originally known as Chapel Street because at No 2 (where Rugby Chambers now stands, opposite the Rugby Arms) was the early eighteenth century Episcopal Chapel of St John. Never consecrated, it nonetheless attracted a number of distinguished Anglican preachers and the congregation included William Wilberforce. It was a strongly Evangelical chapel whose resident preacher, the Rev. Baptist Wriothesley Noel, went off in 1848 to become a Baptist and minister at John Street around the corner, that chapel in turn being another casualty of wartime bombing. Millman Street, which runs north from Rugby Street here, has another concentration of public housing. The writer Gerald Brenan, before Great James Street, once lived at No 10 and another famous lodger, was John Bellingham, a bankrupt from Liverpool with a grudge who set out from Millman Street in 1812 for the lobby of the House of Commons where he assassinated the Prime Minister, Spencer Percival. An outraged House granted a pension to Percival's descendants which eventually came down to the civil servant and patron of the arts in the early twentieth century, Edward Marsh, who used this 'murder money' to purchase art from young painters and launch the famous *Georgian Poetry* anthologies. Marsh lived at the other end of Great James Street, as I've already noted, in Raymond Buildings, Gray's Inn.

Down the side of French's Dairy is what may have the distinction of being Bloomsbury's smallest street, Emerald Court, a tiny passage that will take only one person at a time and which leads through to another narrow street, Emerald Lane, where some eighteenth century boundary markers for the limits of the Bedford Charity can still be seen fixed to the wall. Just here, in the fourteenth century, ran the White Conduit which took water to the Greyfriars Monastery in Newgate Street in the City. At the end of the alley is the marker for another conduit, Lamb's, which is further evidence that good water has always been found here – the pump at Queen Square was always known for the quality of its water. Lamb's Conduit Fields was also known as a place for duelling, a sport alluded to by the character D'Urfey in Wycherley's Restoration Comedy, *Love in a Wood* in 1672 which contains the lines:

> Let him that boasts of too much strength
> Appoint the place and *send his rapier's length.*
>
> ******
>
> Let him that on that basis honour builds,
> Meet me tomorrow in Lamb's Conduit Fields.

William Lamb was an Elizabethan courtier, and a rich member of the Clothworkers' Company, who in 1577 connected several springs to form a head of water that was conveyed by a lead pipe about 2000 yards long to Snow Hill, where he rebuilt for £1500 a derelict conduit there that had fallen out of use, marked by the figure of a lamb, and was duly honoured for his public-spiritedness. In 1667 Lamb's Conduit was rebuilt to a design by Sir Christopher Wren. It lasted until 1746 by which time the New River Company had the monopoly of water supply, having seen off the competition from the now defunct City conduits that had survived the Fire of London, and the new Foundling Hospital was being built on Lamb's Conduit Fields. There is a stone sunk in the wall where Long Yard meets Lamb's Conduit Street that reads: "Lamb's Conduit the Property of the City of London this Pump is Erected for the Benefit of the Publick." The pump is no longer there and the stone lamb, which briefly became the pub sign, long ago vanished, but the surrounding stone is a reminder. As late as 1870, however, when Samuel Palmer wrote his history of St Pancras, the springs were still accessed and were supplying the pumps in Mecklenburgh and Brunswick Squares. Palmer observed: "Lamb's Conduit was one of the many conduits in London which, on days of public rejoicing, were made to run with wine. This mode of pleasing the commonalty was much easier to practise than many suppose; for while the popular notion was that the efflux of wine was the same as that of the water, it was nothing of the sort; a hogshead of wine was put in communication with the conduit and allowed to run out, but the aperture from which the people filled their vessels was never larger than that of a straw."[2]

The 'commonalty' no longer has free wine on fair days but there are two decent pubs within a few yards: The Lamb, a Young's pub with its famous engraved glass moveable little 'snob windows' above the bar around which, or through, or below, one tries to catch the attention of the bar staff, but which were put there to prevent the better sort of patron seeing or being seen by the rough customers of the public bar. The Lamb was originally known as the Lion & Lamb when it opened around 1799, and very close to here would have been the *Jacob's Room* of Virginia Woolf's novel. Opposite used to be Mel Calman's Cartoon Gallery, which I remember from the 1970s. The other pub is the Perseverance, which used to be a more down to earth real ale pub called the Sun (and has in fact run through a number of names in step with rapidly changing fashions in the pub trade, including, bizarrely, the Finnegans Wake at one point in the 1990s) and which is appropriately gentrified in the new Lamb's Conduit Street. In my time the ordinary fruit and vegetable shop in the street disappeared although there is a new organic food shop which is attractive enough if you don't have to worry about money, and a new 'People's Supermarket' is just about to open as I write. The spacious

Ciao Bella Ristorante next to the Lamb has outdoor tables all year round thanks to the sort of heaters which are meant to affront our green conscience, and along the street are wine bars, restaurants, bespoke tailors, a funeral parlour, and several shops so specialist and arcane that one hardly ever sees anyone coming in or out of them and wonders how they survive. In contrast to Marchmont Street which has a kind of rough utilitarian vitality, Lamb's Conduit Street is a more genteel place to saunter and sip a glass of wine and pick at some tapas, and it caters to more refined tastes. One of the most attractive shops in Lamb's Conduit Street is Persephone Books at No 59. Persephone re-issues neglected twentieth century classics, mostly by women, and their books are beautifully produced with simple uniform grey covers, though they occasionally push the boat out with a splash of colour. It's their office premises but there is also a bookshop and a few chairs inside where one can sit and browse.

At No 64 Lamb's Conduit Street, easily missed if you are not looking up, is a striking facade, showing a bundle of fasces, on a building that was once the United Patriots National Benefit Society, which provided sickness cover and life assurance. It was founded in 1843 as the carving says, but originally in North Gower Street.

At the northern end of Lamb's Conduit Street there is big brutalist Holborn Police Station (police are rarely seen on the streets of Bloomsbury, only their deafening sirens shrieking in the night air) which 'aliens' used to have to attend to register. Just across Theobalds Road here (cheating again!) is a real live ordinary butcher's shop excellent for game. In Bloomsbury itself, there are only supermarket meat counters, nor are there any self-standing bakers or fishmongers or fruiterers. Waitrose and Tesco rule. Parisians would be aghast.

Theobalds Road ends at Southampton Row but just before this rears the huge tower block of Unite, the union created in 2009 from a merger of the Transport & General Workers Union and Amicus. No one seems to have noticed that round the corner in Southampton Row there is another Unite, the student halls

of residence company that has some smart new halls in Woburn Place. In the foyer of what was formerly 'the T&G' there are several bronze busts of once legendary figures in the trades union movement. I particularly like one of Frank Cousins, General Secretary of the TGWU from 1956 to 1969 and a minister in Harold Wilson's government in the mid-1960s. It captures perfectly the posture of one of the brothers addressing a meeting, knuckles face downward on the green baize, leaning forward to emphasise his point. Also in the foyer is an abstract sculpture by the wayward Liverpool genius Arthur Dooley, called 'No Pasaran', no doubt welcomed by his fellow-Liverpudlian and Spanish Civil War veteran, the late Jack Jones, General Secretary from 1968 to 1976 and later a powerful campaigner on behalf of pensioners.

Down the right hand side of the Unite building is Boswell Street (formerly Devonshire Street), another of those too-narrow, shaded Bloomsbury streets that are crying out for a bit more light. Half-way down, next to my favourite Italian restaurant, La Porchetta, is Cecil House, a hostel for homeless women, on the site of which, in the years before the First World War, a poetic revolution broke out. No blue plaque will tell you this but here stood Harold Monro's Poetry Bookshop when the street was still known as Devonshire Street. Forgotten now as a poet, Monro's role in the history of early twentieth century poetry is nonetheless secure and it was here in January 1913 that he opened his famous Poetry Bookshop which became the focus for the very contrasting Imagist and Georgian poetic movements just before the First World War. Monro was an evangelical promoter of poetry of all kinds and the Poetry Bookshop, through its publishing activities and readings became the centre of the early-twentieth century poetry scene in London.[3]

In 1913, Devonshire Street was a rough neighbourhood belied by the faded elegance of the Georgian houses, many of which were destroyed during the Blitz. No 35, the bookshop premises, was one of the bombing casualties and drawings show a flat-fronted, pedimented facade, but the area was so dubious that police took the precaution of patrolling it in pairs. Sir Osbert Sitwell described it as "a narrow street [...] rather dark, but given over to screaming children, lusty small boys armed with catapults, and to leaping flights of cats". When he sailed down the road to perform his poetry at the Bookshop, he acquired a following of jeering, derisive kids who mocked his elegant suit and canary-yellow waistcoat. Rupert Brooke, in his trademark broad-brimmed hat, attracted a similar crowd of young people who chanted: "Buffalo Bill! Buffalo Bill!"

Monro chose the shop deliberately because it was within easy reach of literary Bloomsbury, the universities, and the art schools. The house next door was occupied by a large, noisy woman who kept a flower stall at Piccadilly Circus. Her yobbish sons, when presented by Monro with one of the illustrated children's books he published, promptly tore them into small pieces and stamped them into the ground. On the other side of the shop was a goldbeaters' workshop, now La Porchetta. Browsers in the Bookshop could hear the regular beat of the goldbeaters' hammers coming through the wall as they read the latest publications by Eliot or Pound. On the upper floors were some rooms that Monro let out to deserving artists and poets like the sculptor Jacob Epstein or the poet T.E. Hulme. Wilfred Owen, after he had just signed up to fight, tried to get digs here while training round the corner at the Drill Hall, but he was disappointed and had to rent a room above the coffee shop opposite. The Poetry Bookshop readings were held in an annexe behind the house (another former goldbeaters' workshop), dimly and theatrically lit, and the performers included T.S. Eliot, Robert Graves, Ezra Pound, Walter de la Mare, and just about every significant poet of the era. When W.B. Yeats performed he was such a draw that the reading was staged instead at the Artificers' Guild Hall (today's Art Workers' Guild) a hundred yards away in Queen Square.

As well as being a poetry bookshop and a publishing house and a centre for lovers of poetry, 35 Devonshire Street was also a kind of evangelical centre of the avant-garde and it was here, on the night of 11th July 1913, after the first London performance of Stravinsky's *Le Sacre du printemps*, that anyone who was anyone in the new poetry scene in London gathered to celebrate the glorious rout of the Philistines. A modernist explosion had been detonated and everyone was delirious. Looking at this rather colourless corner of Bloomsbury today it is perhaps a little hard to imagine this vivacious scene.

The Poetry Bookshop continued to thrive after the First World War until the lease ran out in 1926. Helped by a loan from Monro's mother, the shop moved to new premises at No 38 Great Russell Street, with an entrance around the side in Willoughby Street.[4] Still keen to cock a snook at the philistines, Monro commissioned from the Art Deco American poster artist Edward McKnight Kauffer a bright, futuristic shop-sign showing an illuminated book and a lyre. The Duke of Bedford disliked the way the sign projected, as well as the bright-red window frames Monro had painted. He ordered that they be re-painted in a dull white to conform with the rest of the block. The Poetry Bookshop continued to trade until June 1935 and its premises are now Munchkin's Fish and Chip Shop, very popular with overseas visitors to the British Museum, especially as they accept payment in dollars and yen.

As well as poets and goldbeaters, Boswell Street was home to many poor Italian ice-cream vendors, organ-grinders and chestnut-sellers until the Second World War and it still remains very cosmopolitan though the predominant ethnic group now is probably Bangladeshi rather than Italian.

A few yards further north, Boswell Street opens out into Queen Square. Eighteenth century engravings show Queen Square open on its northern side with fields stretching unimpeded to the hills of Hampstead and Highgate in the distance but today it is closed, with only pedestrian alleys allowing one to leave the north end of the Square, which contributes to its secluded air. In the south-western corner is the church of St George-the-Martyr where on 16th June 1956 (the day James Joyce fans celebrate as 'Bloomsday') Ted Hughes and Sylvia Plath, as already noted, were married in what Hughes called 'St George of the Chimney Sweeps', recalling how they exchanged rings in "that echo-gaunt, weekday chancel". St George-the-Martyr was erected in 1706 as a chapel-of-ease to St Andrew's Holborn. It was named after Sir Streynsham Master, the first Governor of St George, the nucleus of the City of Madras, and Master was behind the plan to recoup the building costs by renting

out pews. It became a separate parish in 1723 when some additions were made to it by Nicholas Hawksmoor. It was originally a plain brick building that the eighteenth century London historian John Noorthouck called "void of all elegance"[5]. The antiquarian William Stukeley, who in 1747 became rector of St George's, and whose eccentric obsessions meant, according to one nineteenth century historian, that he "sometimes allowed his speculations to be unduly influenced by his imagination"[6], kept a rural retreat two and a half miles to the north at Kentish Town: "an half-hour's walk over sweet fields. 'Tis absolutely and clearly out of the influence of the London smoak, a dry gravelly soil, and air remarkably wholesome."[7] Stukeley's batty theories about Stonehenge earned him the nickname 'The Arch-Druid'. The church is sometimes called 'The Chimney Sweeps' Church' because of a charitable dinner that used to be held there every Christmas for sweeps' apprentices (the ones who were sent to climb up chimneys and became a symbol of the iniquities of Victorian child labour before the practice was outlawed in 1875). Today it holds free lunchtime concerts in its spacious interior, giving an opportunity to reflect on its eighteenth century décor with Victorian 'improvement' and bits of Gothic overlaying the classical foundation.

Queen Square (originally Devonshire Square and started in 1686 on the area known generally as Lamb's Conduit Fields) is now dwarfed by the hospitals on its eastern side. In the attractive central gardens office workers fill the benches and sprawl on the grass with their sandwiches while pigeons and the occasional magpie waddle about. A small brass tablet in the ground, easy to miss and spattered with pigeon-droppings, says that: "On the night of the eighth of September 1915 a Zeppelin bomb fell and exploded on this spot although nearly one thousand people slept in the surrounding buildings no person was injured." On 24th September 1915 in nearby Southampton Row they were not so lucky. Thirteen people died and 22 were injured on the steps of the old Bedford Hotel by a 112 pound bomb dropped by a Gotha on one of the first night air raids on London. A tablet on the wall of the new Bedford Hotel records this incident. Another plaque in the ground at the southern end of the gardens commemorates the Queen's Jubilee of 1977 with verses by two Faber poets, and fervent non-republicans, Ted Hughes and Philip Larkin.

While the workers relax, relatives wheel along the paths patients from the National Hospital for Neurology and Neurosurgery or the

Royal Homeopathic Hospital or the Hospital for Sick Children in Great Ormond Street. Most of these hospitals began in private houses before the nineteenth century buildings were constructed, but it is only on the western side that one can see how it all must have looked. At No 6 the Art Worker's Guild, where the walls of the main reception room are smothered in portraits of nineenth century arts and crafts household names, and where the writers' organisation English P.E.N. has its Christmas parties, is the finest example of a late-eighteenth century house, just a few doors away from the former Faber and Faber bunker which is currently being rebuilt. Also on that western side, on the opposite corner of Cosmo Place to St George-the-Martyr, is the Queen's Larder, a fine little pub whose landlord has been waging for some time a very successful war against the *faux*-jolly tradition of pub landlords. Who needs a smile when the beer and the ambience is so pleasant. Cosmo Place itself is a little pedestrianised walk connecting Queens Square to Southampton Row, and containing another pub eighteenth century in origin, The Swan, a couple of cheap Italian restaurants, and Cosmo China, where a collective of craftswomen make bright and original hand-made ceramics they will personalise for you as special gifts.

On the south side of Queen Square the Mary Ward Centre is a big Georgian house, before the First World War the site of the Government School of Art for Ladies, that is now an adult educational centre where I acquired my City and Guilds Certificate in Preparing to Teach in the Lifelong Learning Centre – worth doing a course just to taste the delicious food in its café. Next to it is the former Italian Hospital (founded by Giovanni Ortelli in 1884 for Italian immigrants but since 1989 part of Great Ormond Street Hospital). Along the eastern side, which is wall-to-wall hospital building, once stood the house where William Morris had his weaving-workshop from 1865 at what was No 25. Coming from Red Lion Square, Morris & Co had its headquarters here for the next seventeen years. Like so many Bloomsbury businesses Morris worked with the

constraints of a Georgian house to convert it into an office and show-room on the ground floor and turned the former ballroom at the back, which was connected to the main house by a wooden gallery, into the chief workshop. More overspill workshops were in time built in the yards at the rear and in Ormond Yard. While he was here launching his new tapestry-weaving line, William Morris wrote *The Life and Death of Jason* and *The Earthly Paradise.* No 25 had previously been, with No 24, a "seminary for young ladies" nicknamed 'The Ladies' Eton' and rumoured to contain in one of the rooms a carriage which enabled the young ladies to practise getting in and out of one gracefully. At No 22 a slightly less elevated clientele attended the Ladies' Charity School founded for "educating, clothing, and maintaining the daughters of respectable parents in reduced and necessitous circumstances" as its 1702 founding article put it.

On this side too in the eighteenth century was the well-known Golden Head bookseller's shop, and Alderman Barber, a good friend of Jonathan Swift and later Lord Mayor of London in 1732, lived in the Square as did the novelist Fanny Burney who wrote of her father, Dr Burney's, house at No 39: "A beautiful prospect of the hills ever verdant of Hampstead and Highgate, at that time faced the Doctor's dwelling in Queen Square."[8] Dr Johnson's friend Dr John Campbell was another resident until he died there in 1775 and Johnson went there most Sunday evenings until he became fed up with "the shoals of Scotchmen who flocked about him". But all this is buried under the hospitals which began to be established in the second half of the nineteenth century with names like the Hospital for Hip Diseases in Childhood (1867) and the Hospital for the Paralysed and Epileptic (1881). At No 29 was the Working Women's College, founded by Elizabeth Malleson in 1864 after the Working Men's College baulked at admitting women. F.D. Maurice, co-founder of the Working Men's College lived for a time at No 20. The poor law and workhouse reformer, Louisa Twining also lived at No 20, as did the architect Thomas Wyatt, but by 1907 it had become a Quaker institute. This was the location, mentioned earlier, of the mediaeval conduit – variously known as the Devil's Conduit and Chimney Conduit – that became the site of the Turkish Baths. In the north east corner of the Square a blue plaque was unveiled in 2010 on the wall of the residential block, Queen Court, to commemorate Wing Commander Forest Frederick Edward Yeo-Thomas, who, in addition to having a lot of first names, was one of the most courageous RAF secret agents of the

Second World War, codenamed 'The White Rabbit', and who lived here after the war.

At the northern end of the square, on the flagstones in front of the Mary Ward Centre, a redundant pump, later a gas lamp, is preserved behind the fruiterer's stall and is a reminder that the water here was once renowned. The Rev. E.C. Bedford, a nineteenth century rector of St George-the-Martyr wrote: "It was a sight to see the procession of jug-carrying servants from the great houses, and children from the poorer houses, making their way to the pump each day."[9] Queen Square, like so many other Bloomsbury Squares, made the gradual transition from exclusive residential area to institutional or commercial and office use. In 1820 a Queen Square resident was said to have remarked: "When I came to the square I was the only lady in it who did not keep a carriage. Before I left I was the only one who did."

Coming out of Cosmo Place into Southampton Row a plaque on the hotel on the corner tells that Sir John Barbarolli, the great conductor, was born in a house on the site. His father was a member of the orchestra at the Holborn Empire. Along here, in the 1960s (again, hard to credit that such a counter-cultural phenomenon would have chosen a staid location such as this) were the offices of *International Times*. In his account of those days in his book *In the Sixties,* Barry Miles describes the foundation of the legendary Indica Bookshop at 102 Southampton Row. Formerly it was a bookshop called Jackson's, which sold school books, a lot of them to missionary schools in Africa and to convents, but also attracted some of the Bloomsbury intellectuals. A visitor's book survives with signatures from Huxley, Keynes and other members of the Bloomsbury Group. Indica opened in 1966 and the premises consisted of numerous small rooms amounting to 2,700 square feet in all. "The top shelves," Miles recalls, "housed concealed lighting and Melonex was stretched across the room between the tops of the bookcases to make a shimmering silver ceiling, inspired by Andy Warhol's Factory, except that our silver surface would move every time someone opened the door."[10]

Indica had new headed notepaper "featuring the Mayan flying-saucer figure discovered at Paleneque" and launched with panache, surviving until its liquidation in 1969. The subversive *International Times,* or *IT* as it was better known, was planned in the Kardomah café in Southampton Row where Miles and the prospective editor Tom McGrath used to sit amongst the tweedy ladies from the shires up in town for the shopping. It wasn't a conventional editorial office: "Michael X and Howard Parker, known as 'H', Jimi Hendrix's roadie, used to stay up all night taking acid in our kitchen, seated one at each end of the glass dining table.... We used to go off to bed and leave them to it. In the morning they'd still be there, nodding and grinning." But it was a fine location, with the front windows of Miles's flat over the shop looking out over the dome of the British Museum and, a little further to the west, cranes were lifting up into position the Y-shaped components of Centre Point, Richard Seifert's modernist high rise, which according to Miles had the effect of causing planning blight all down Charing Cross Road for the next two decades.

IT had an office in the basement of No 102 and paid its rent in copies of the paper. Office equipment was a little minimal but they did have an ancient typewriter donated by Sonia Orwell which was supposedly used by George himself. The paper was launched on 11th October 1966 at the Roundhouse, Chalk Farm, and an obscure band called Pink Floyd provided the music. Or as *The Sunday Times* reported: "a pop group called the Pink Floyd played throbbing music while a series of bizarre coloured shapes flashed on a huge screen behind them".

Back in Queen Square and leaving it on the eastern side this time by turning into Great Ormond Street, the famous Hospital for Children dominates the entire length of the street on the northern side as far as its intersection with Lamb's Conduit Street. Anxious parents pace up and down and sometimes, when some high-risk operation such as the separation of Siamese twins is taking place, there are news crews and photographers also killing time on the pavement outside, waiting for a bulletin. Halfway down on the other side, a tiny alley opens off, Barbon Close, commemorating a notorious seventeenth century speculative developer, Nicholas Barbon, son of Praisegod Barebone who gave his name to the Barebone's Parliament at the time of the English Civil War. Barbon's biggest scheme was Red Lion Square. Just beyond this was, until very recently, the tiniest second hand bookshop in Bloomsbury, Griffith & Partners, much-lamented and now the premises of the Espresso Room – probably the tiniest coffee shop in Bloomsbury! The extinction of second hand book dealers in Bloomsbury is a melancholy story but, fortunately, as I have shown already, there are a good few left.

CORAM'S FIELDS

At the northern end of Lamb's Conduit Street I find myself facing what is left of The Foundling Hospital, set in the middle of Coram's Fields. As I approach the railings in front of this large open space which preserves, to some extent, the "plain but ample" shape, as Pevsner has it, of the original mid-eighteenth century Foundling Hospital building which was demolished in 1926. A notice on the railings says that adults are not permitted inside the grounds unless accompanied by a child. This prohibition long preceded the current British hysteria about adults having any sort of contact with children and reflects the fact that, though the Hospital has gone, the site is still occupied by the splendid Thomas Coram Foundation which works with what they call "vulnerable children, young people and their families, transforming their lives through practical help and support. We aim to build self-esteem and well-being, preparing children and young people for a fulfilling adult life". At night floodlights illuminate the hard surface football pitches and the Foundation – one of the oldest charities in Britain and the first founded explicitly for children in 1739 – is clearly thriving today in its spacious grounds. Down the western side, facing Lansdowne Terrace, are the educational flower and herb beds and there is an occasional sighting of the pet sheep, which, on hot summer days when they are dirty and dusty, seem to be pining for real pasture somewhere.

Captain Thomas Coram sailor and shipwright who, after he had returned from years at sea, was appalled by what he saw in early eighteenth century London: unwanted children flung to die on dung heaps, and he resolved to found a charity to rescue them. There was plenty of space to accommodate the large Foundling Hospital and contemporary engravings show a grand approach flanked by two wings (east for the girls, west for the boys). The author of *Lost London*, Hermione Hobhouse, calls the 1926 demolition, when the Hospital was moved out to

Hertfordshire where it never thrived, "tragic"[11] and points out that the site would have been much more appropriate as the site of London University, something being actively canvassed in the 1920s at the time of its destruction. This would have had the additional advantage of preserving much of residential Bloomsbury which was poised to disappear under the University bulldozers. The site was in fact selected to become the new Covent Garden Market and a Bill to that effect was introduced in Parliament in 1926 but, after a campaign by Lord Rothermere's *Daily Mail* and much public protest, the site was bought back by a trust headed by Lord Rothermere and leased in perpetuity for the recreation and education of children. The Foundling Chapel, where Handel performed his *Messiah* in aid of the Hospital funds, with its original high box pews and ornate plasterwork, was also swept away in 1926.

All that remains now, apart from the contemporary Coram charity buildings, is a 1937 neo-Georgian building at No 40 Brunswick Square that houses the Foundling Museum – which often mounts imaginative exhibitions that place contemporary artists like Tracey Emin or Paula Rego alongside the treasures of the permanent collection like Hogarth's 'March of the Guards to Finchley' (1749) mentioned earlier, and Sophia Anderson's touching late-Victorian picture of 'Foundling Girls at Prayer in the Chapel' which shows the girls in their white aprons and distinctive white linen caps. At the time of the Hospital's foundation London had no public art galleries and, by persuading distinguished artists like Hogarth, one of the first governors of the Hospital, to donate works, Coram effectively sowed the seed of permanent art gallery institutions like the Royal Academy of Arts. Hogarth himself leaned on many of his fellow artists who often became governors after they had donated paintings. Handel was another distinguished benefactor and the museum today has a good collection of material relating to Handel, whose music one can listen to in large comfy armchairs in a special room at the top of the house. No 40 has managed to rescue some items from the original

Hospital building such as the heavy oak staircase from the Boys' Wing and some rococo ceilings. It also presents a very informative history of the Hospital through many interesting and moving exhibits. Captain Coram, who realised his dream, but who seems to have fallen out with the Hospital governors in the end, dying a poor man in 1751, is immortalised in a statue outside the current museum.

Captain Coram's original plans for the Foundling Hospital were far from plain sailing. Earlier plans for such a charity had been abandoned in Queen Anne's reign on the grounds that provision for illegitimate children might actually serve to increase the likelihood of their being engendered, but he prevailed and the first house for foundlings was actually opened in Hatton Garden on 26th October 1740, the year after a Royal Charter was granted to the Foundation. The previous day a notice had been fixed to the door to say that 20 children would be admitted under the following conditions:

1. No child exceeding the age of two months will be taken in, nor such as have the evil, leprosy of diseases of that nature.
2. The person who brings a child is to come at the outward door and ring a bell at the inward door, and not to go away until the child is returned or notice given of its reception; but no questions whatever will be asked of any person bringing a child, nor shall any servant of the house presume to endeavour to discover who such person is, on pain of being at once discharged.
3. All persons who bring children are requested to affix on each child some particular writing or other distinguishing mark or token, so that the children may be known if hereafter necessary.[12]

When a sign quickly appeared saying 'The House is Full' there were fights and many of the infants were seriously injured so a ballot was introduced instead, in the additional hope that it would help those "weak and sickly women" who could not fight. Because so many came forward a new plot of ground was purchased on Lamb's Conduit Fields and this became known as the Foundling Estate. Actually sifting applicants remained a problem and the next idea to solve it was to hang a basket at the gate with the instruction that the parent or nurse, on depositing their burdens in the basket, should ring the bell and depart. Within three years, however, this system was creaking under the strain after more than 15,000 infants were deposited. In fact the existence of this facility led amoral entrepreneurs to organise a regular traffic in children, as poor people from all over Britain discovered a way of disposing of unwanted children in the confidence that they would be carefully tended and brought up. The historian Samuel Palmer quoted an example of four children sent from Yorkshire in two panniers across a horse's back at eight guineas a trip: "On arriving at the gate of the hospital, these carriers used literally to strip the little things naked, for the value of their clothing, before they deposited them in the basket." This forced the Hospital governors to come up with another idea, which was to charge £100 for depositing a child but it "was considered to be making the charity a receptacle for the bastard children of the nobility, therefore in 1801 this mode was abolished." In the end the modern method of making a proper assessment of applications from the parent was preferred.

Parents often left a token of some kind (samples can be seen in the museum today) to identify their child (and prove to others that they had not committed infanticide). Tokens included coins, playing cards with messages or simple verses written on them like: "You have my heart;/Though we must part." One wealthy banker, however, trying later in life to excavate his past as a Foundling boy, drew a blank probably because he was one of the babies stripped of everything as he swung in the overnight basket. Since many of the first boys taken in were destined for the navy (the girls for service), the very first males were given the surnames of well-known admirals such as Drake and Blake. Later, apprenticeship was what normally followed their discharge.

MECKLENBURGH SQUARE

At the northern end of Lamb's Conduit Street, facing Coram's Fields, is one of those sad metropolitan sights, marooned in the middle of a traffic island, a defunct underground Victorian public lavatory. These splendid subterranean palaces ought to be brought back into use. Wake up Camden Council! In front of this one is a fountain, also defunct, of a girl, kneeling and pouring water from a jug in allusion to Lamb's Conduit. Known as the Francis Whiting Fountain this is also a reminder that the whole of Guilford Street that runs west to east here was built on the banks of a tributary of the now buried Fleet river. Mecklenburgh Square, which was designed in 1808 by Joseph Kay, Surveyor to the Foundling Estate, lies just off Guilford Street. Though heavily damaged by World War Two

bombing, it is an easily overlooked example of the grand Bloomsbury style, especially the eastern side which opens out a grand vista towards Doughty Street to the south. It was designed to balance Brunswick Square to the west, both squares flanking the Foundling Hospital, and today it seems to have been colonised by a large educational foundation, Henry Goodenough. Goodenough College describes itself as "an independent college for international postgraduate students" and has over 600 members from 90 countries. It offers accommodation and private access to Mecklenburgh Square. In 2011 the College will be celebrating its 80th anniversary, having originally been established in the 1930s as a postgraduate residential institution for students from what were known in those days as 'the Dominions'.

The eastern side of Mecklenburgh Square is the most impressive, a wall of very grand houses spattered with blue plaques, including one to the socialist author of *The Acquisitive Society* (1921) R.H. Tawney and one to the Muslim scholar, Sir Syed Ahmed Khan (1817-98). In 1938 Graham Greene rented a studio here, while writing *The Confidential Agent* and *The Power and the Glory*. He maintained that Welsh was often heard spoken in the Portland Arms (long ago demolished) on the corner of Millman Street, and the London Welsh Association used to be based at No 11, with access to the London Welsh Centre in Gray's Inn Road behind. On the northern side of the Square at No 44, during the First World War, lived the Imagist poet, Hilda Dolittle, known as H.D. Married to Richard Aldington, whose novel *Death of a Hero* was much acclaimed as a bitter commentary on the futility of war, H.D.'s own novel, *Bid Me to Live* (which I find a more considerable work of art than Aldington's, powerful as his depictions of war undoubtedly are) was set in part in Mecklenburgh Square which she disguises as "Queen's Square" – confusingly because Queen Square (without the apostrophe) is not far away. She evokes a cold Bloomsbury sitting room inhabited by her heroine in 1917 and 1918 (the book is autobiographical) while her husband is away at the Front and shows how the pain of war was felt at home as well as in the trenches. Even today there is something rather cold about this square, in spite of its attractive remaining architecture, perhaps because it is so large and so dominated by institutions and the central garden, being private, prevents any spontaneous gathering of people, any animation, such as one has in abundance in Russell Square or Queen Square. This is Haughty rather than Demotic Bloomsbury.

ORDINARY PEOPLE

Back in Guilford Street I try to recall Thackeray's *The Ballad of Eliza Davis* which immortalises No 24, now buried under a bland university block:

> In this street there lived a housemaid,
> If you particularly ask me where –
> Vy, it was at four and twenty
> Guildford Street by Brunswick Square.

The same ballad refers also to the Foundling Hospital:

> P'haps you know the Fondling Chapel,
> Where the little children sings?
> Lord! I like to hear, on Sundays,
> Them there pretty little things.

Thackeray was another of Bloomsbury's famous literary inhabitants but it is easy to forget that the area still has a considerable population today of people who are not fashionable metropolitan writers and dons, celebrities and architects, but working people living on ordinary council housing estates.

Some of these are very skilfully hidden, like the Dombey Street Estate, one of the first blocks to be built after the war and finished in 1948. Ian Nairn in *Modern Buildings in London* (1964) said of the Dombey Street flats "they have gone grim now" but, given the general condition of public housing in London, they don't seem too bad. Nairn also said: "they were built with a kind of inner integrity that ennobles the grimness, a kind of unselfconscious statement: 'this is how it is; there wasn't much money, but we did our best'." That captures, I think, the decent flavour of this kind of housing. The

Dombey Street Estate nestles away behind Theobalds Road and Lamb's Conduit Street, its tower blocks invisible to the casual *flâneur* who cradles a pint of Young's outside the Lamb public house, or makes a fuss about 'Snowdonia Cheddar', as the posh lady in the organic food shop in Lamb's Conduit Street was doing the other day, as if her life depended on getting exactly the right source of this geography-defying cheese. These Camden Council estates are quite attractive in their way, with pleasant rose-gardens. At least one here has managed to preserve, uniquely, the name of William Blemund: the Blemundsbury Estate. For as long as housing like this remains in public ownership people other than the toffs will have the chance to live in Bloomsbury if they want to.

CROMER STREET MASSIVE

North of the Foundling Estate, off Judd Street, to turn into Cromer Street is to enter another community, that of the Bengalis who live in large numbers between here and King's Cross. Overall Camden has one of the largest proportions of Bangladeshi families in the UK and social surveys indicate that they are a relatively deprived community. In the past there have been some racial attacks which provoked the formation of a gang called Cromer Street Massive, of Bangladeshi origin. I have never seen them but, one evening, my wife was walking back from King's Cross and witnessed a pitched battle between youths wielding chair-legs. I often stroll through the area as a short cut to King's Cross and all one sees are peaceable people sitting outside The Boot public house or chatting outside the Halal butchers or the sari shops. This is not at all a violent ghetto. No doubt there is racial tension under the surface here that I don't see, but it doesn't *feel* rough. The King's Cross Bengali community established itself in the 1950s and 1960s, many were sailors and their families, and it is an integral part of the local community. The Boot was originally the Golden Boot before 1800 and had bowling greens attached. It figures in Dickens's *Barnaby Rudge* as the base for a gang of troublemakers in the Gordon Riots in 1780.

Cromer Street was originally called Lucas Street after its developer Joseph Lucas, a Long Acre tinplate worker who had inherited some cow pasture here where the Peperfield Housing Estate block now stands. The name Peperfield could be an allusion to the watercress which flourished here, as it did on the Long Fields north of Great

Russell Street, from the water leaking from the elmwood pipes of the eighteenth century New River Company. The New River created in the seventeenth century to bring water from Hertfordshire into London, and owned by the New River Company, eventually came under the aegis of the Metropolitan Water Board in 1902 and Thames Water in 1973. The New River is still part of London's water supply system.

The Anglo-Catholic Holy Cross Church in Cromer Street ('The Church in the Heart of King's Cross') defines its mission as "the identification and care of all those whose lives are bound up with King's Cross for whatever reason, and especially those who experience the ravages of life." There are certainly plenty of people in this eastern part of Bloomsbury who look as though "the ravages of life" might have passed over them but fewer now that King's Cross has been cleaned up, the ravaged exported somewhere else. The pubs here, like the warm and friendly McGlynns (before 1996 The Duke of Wellington, the 1990s having seen a rash of Irish theme pubs breaking out in the capital) in Whidborne Street, off Cromer Street, with its good value food and reasonably-priced beer are what one would expect in the heart of a working class community living in public housing, far from the literary and academic salons of *Echt*-Bloomsbury.

THE ZULUS AND TWERPS OF REGENT SQUARE

Early in January 1921, the young Aldous Huxley, whose wife and young son were staying with her family in Belgium, came to lodge for four months at the flat in No 36 Regent Square, south of Cromer Street, leased by T.W. ('Tommy') Earp, a legendary Oxford figure in his day, with another Oxford friend, Russell Green. If you believe Tolkien, T.W. Earp is the derivation of the word 'twerp', but some think he may have been joking. Only one side of Regent Square survived bombing and that strip of Georgian terraced housing on the south side today is not where the young literati lodged. The site of No 36 is now covered by yet more public housing. The fourth member of the household was the (literally) pugnacious South African poet, Roy Campbell, who was later to become the scourge of Bloomsbury. Calling himself 'the Zulu' because of his South African origins and

contempt for mild Oxford manners, Campbell once punched Stephen Spender in the face at a poetry reading and scrapped in the pub with Louis MacNeice. He was contemptuous of Huxley's scientific progressivism as he saw it (though actually both writers would come to share a lack of faith in progressive utopias) and mocked his flatmate as "a pedant who leeringly gloated over his knowledge of how crayfish copulated (through their third pair of legs) but could never have cooked one, let alone broken in a horse, thrown and branded a steer, flensed a whale, or slaughtered, cut, cured, and cooked anything at all".[13] All four young writers had to contend with that well-known handicap of Bloomsbury flat-life: the people upstairs. In this case two young ladies who gave dancing lessons in the flat above. Sent by his flatmates to complain, Russell Green, in his best Oxford polysyllabic manner asked them, when they opened the door, to desist from their 'bombinations'. Outraged, because they thought they heard him say 'abominations', and seeing themselves accused of running a disorderly house, the girls and their dancing-pupils pursued the young man with screams down the stairs.[14]

Campbell would publish, ten years later, his rumbustious satire on Bloomsbury, *The Georgiad* (1931), in muscular rhyming couplets reminiscent of Dryden but, in my view, lacking the earlier satirist's bite. Campbell's sympathetic and insightful biographer, Joseph Pearce, argues that this satire is vitiated by its unnecessary bile but I find the poem – an immaculate first edition of which I plucked out of the late Griffiths & Partners second hand book barrow in Great Ormond Street a few years ago for £1 – actually lacking in the kind of *specificity*, the vivid detail, that makes for the best satire. Highly accomplished as Campbell was as a composer of metrical verse his tilts at the fake rusticity of the Georgian poets and the tedium of literary dinners could, for my taste, have been even more savage. What motivated Campbell's hatred of Bloomsbury was not so much his well-advertised preference for 'ordinary people' – bullfighters, peasants, cow-hands – as the more pertinent fact that his wife Mary had an affair with Vita Sackville-West, the shock of the discovery sending him spinning out of England to settle in Martigues in Provence (though they were reconciled and spent the rest of their lives together). Campbell later converted to Catholicism, translated the Spanish mystic John of the Cross, and polished his hatred of the contemporary world. He blamed the progressive literary intellectuals of Bloomsbury, and their "sex-socialism" for creating a self-indulgent, emotionally shallow and materialistic world, bloodless and lacking in spiritual value. As he thundered in *The Georgiad*:

> They hatch Utopias from their dusty brains
> Which are but Hells, where endless boredom reigns –
> Middle-class Hells, built on a cheap, clean plan,
> Edens of abnegation, dread to scan,
> Founded upon a universal ban:
> For banned from thence is all that fires or thrills,
> Pain, vengeance, danger, or the clash of wills...[15]

This was a common depiction of Bloomsbury as a collection of smug idealists whose private incomes and social superiority insulated them from the harsher realities of life – and contact with the lower orders whose fate they pretended to be concerned for. As I shall argue later, when discussing the Bloomsbury Group in detail, there is some truth in this. Abhorring the sweaty workmen who came to install the central heating at her pile in Sissinghurst, Vita Sackville-West exclaimed: "My God how workmen smell! The whole house stinks of them. I hate the proletariat." Campbell's close friend and drinking-companion, Dylan Thomas, shared his contempt for "the shams and shamans, the amateur hobo and homo of Bloomsbury, W.C.1".[16]

The remaining terrace of houses in Regent Square includes No 6 where the artist William Coldstream lived in the 1920s and 1930s. He was co-founder of the Euston Road School of painters, a movement to restore the virtues of realism in painting, and later Professor of Fine Art at the Slade School, University College. Regent Square was particularly badly hit by wartime bombing in the 1940s with St Peter's Greek revival church (by the same architects who designed St Pancras Church) being destroyed (though its Ionic portico lingered on until 1967) and the Gothic National Scotch Church which was replaced by the Regent Square United Reformed Church.

I began by proposing that Bloomsbury had the flavour of an urban village, a genuine community in the heart of the capital. I meant that even in the city centre, patterns of attachment and familiar daily ritual exist that tie people to a sense of place, a fondness for their 'patch', but it would be wrong to suggest that Bloomsbury is homogeneous. Passing Argyle Street Primary School at the end of the school day, and watching the jumping, shouting, laughing cascade of almost wholly Asian kids tumble out of the old-fashioned Victorian exit, one really does wonder what connection they might feel with the rather dry and haughty world of University and Intellectual Bloomsbury to the west.

Notes

1. Philip Thomas, *Our Church and Faith of Humanity: An Opening Discourse Delivered at the Church of Humanity, Chapel Street, Holborn on the 9th Day of the Month of Moses in the year 56 of the Positivist Era (Being the 9th January, 1910 of the Christian Era)* (1910), p4
2. Samuel Palmer, *Old St Pancras* (1870), p91
3. For a fuller account of this period and the role of Harold Monro see, Nicholas Murray, *The Red Sweet Wine of Youth* (2011), Chapter One.
4. For a full history see Joy Grant, *Harold Monro and the Poetry Bookshop* (1967)
5. John Noorthouck, *A New History of London* (1773), p745
6. George Clinch, *Bloomsbury and St Giles* (1890) p190
7. Diary of William Stukely quoted by Gillian Tindall in *The Fields Beneath* ,p91
8. Cited by Philip Norman, 'Queen Square, Bloomsbury, and its Neighbourhood', *London Topographical Record,* Vol X (1916), p 5
9. Quoted by Norman, p13
10. Barry Miles, *In the Sixties* (2002), p126
11. Hermione Hobhouse, *Lost London: a Century of Demolition and Decay* (1976), p142
12. Reproduced by Samuel Palmer, op. cit., p233
13. Quoted in Nicholas Murray, *Aldous Huxley: an English Intellectual* (2003), p126
14. Roy Campbell, *Light on a Dark Horse* (1971), p194
15. Roy Campbell, *The Georgiad* (1931), p39
16. Paul Ferris (ed.) *The Collected Letters of Dylan Thomas* (1985), p56

WEST

BEDFORD SQUARE

It's a crisp March afternoon and I am standing outside Congress House, the headquarters of the Trades Union Congress in Great Russell Street, under an entrance canopy that supports a vast sculpture by Bernard Meadows, 'The Spirit of Brotherhood'. Inside, in the inner courtyard, is a Jacob Epstein sculpture from 1955 commemorating trade unionists who died in two world wars. Today I am the guest of Tony McDonnell, a London Blue Badge Guide who is taking out a group of overseas academics on a Bloomsbury walk. The Blue Badge Guides are formidably prepared and have to study for two years, like cab drivers acquiring 'the knowledge', and take an exam before they are let loose on the visiting public. I am going to learn a lot on this walk. Tony is well briefed and tailors his patter to the academic audience in tow, who want to hear about 'Bloomsbury' and its lives and loves. There's a whisper that some of the distinguished foreign guests are dubious about embarking on a walk because, where they come from, it's only the poor who move about on foot, but they muck in and there's the promise of dinner at the Fitzroy Tavern at the end of it all. I am honoured to be allowed to come along.

There's a nice bristle of blue and bronze plaques opposite the TUC to get us going. Thanet House, currently the headquarters of the English Speaking Union, is on the site of the original Thanet House where the Earl of Thanet, and later the Earl of Leicester, lived. One of the plaques, at No 100, marks the residence of Topham Beauclerk an eighteenth century friend of Dr Johnson married to Lady Diana Beauclerk (the original Lady Di) which provokes a murmur of interest. Another plaque at No 105-6 marks the fact that the architects Pugin, father and son, lived here. We are due to turn into Adeline Place, heading for Bedford Square, but first a genuflection at No 14, the only one of the original eighteenth century houses that remains in Great Russell Street, and another Dickens site. Charles Kitterbell, who features in the *Sketches by Boz*, in the chapter 'The Bloomsbury Christening', lived in a house here whose address he gave as Bedford Square unlike his Uncle Dumps who "always dropped the 'Bedford Square', and inserted in lieu thereof, the dreadful words, 'Tottenham Court Road'." Next door to No 14 are the premises of Mr Topper, who sounds like another Dickensian character, but who is in fact a chain of cheap hairdressers with several outlets in central London. They used to advertise haircuts for £5 but time and inflation have moved on and it is now £7. Though I am the grandson of an eminent Bootle barber I always hate getting my hair cut and the real attraction of Mr Topper as opposed to Vidal Sassoon is that it is *very quick*. You can sometimes be in and out in ten minutes which, though ten minutes too long for me, is a lot less than it would be anywhere else. The cutters are all young people from all over the world, and you feel that they are just about to hoist up a backpack and move on. Because they are young they are recently trained, so they always do a first rate job. Why pay more?

Our little platoon is moving towards Bedford Square. The author of *Eats, Shoots and Leaves* lives just round here so I must be careful about my grammar. Entering Bedford Square one is reminded once again what a perfect example of the eighteenth century Bloomsbury Square it is. Easily the best-preserved of all the squares, it is complete on all four sides with a prominent pedimented central building rearing in the middle of each of those sides. First constructed in 1775-86, on a site known as 'St Giles ruins' where The Rookery once stood, it was intended to attract the aristocracy but in the end most of the first inhabitants were lawyers, drawn by the proximity of the Inns of Court. The fourth Duke of Bedford had big plans for a vast circus like that at Bath but the architect, Thomas Leverton, settled for a more restrained pattern of grand but not flashy houses. The first two leases were taken by the Duchess of Bedford and the Duchess of Marlborough and the Duke's right hand man Robert Palmer. Lessees were forbidden to do anything on the premises which "may be or grow to the annoyance, grievance, damage or disturbance of the said duchesses and Robert Palmer or their heirs" and this prohibition might explain the slightly bossy attitude of the Bedford Estate ever since. Stringent requirements were imposed on the builders and they had to use Portland Stone, lead gutters and pipes and slate for roofs and the door cases were made of the artificial Coade stone, manufactured in Lambeth to a secret formula that was subsequently lost. The famous 'South Bank Lion' on the south end of Westminster Bridge

today was made of the same artificial stone, a form of glazed terracotta.

In spite of all this care, however, the aristos didn't come in numbers. Mayfair was still considered posher than Bloomsbury and at the end of the eighteenth century there were sixteen members of the aristocracy living in Berkeley Square while Bedford Square could now offer only two lords. During the nineteenth century, it was favoured by lawyers, doctors and architects, with actors appearing later in the century. The Lord Chancellor, Lord Eldon, lived at No 6, one of the grandest houses in the Square on the eastern side but when the Bedford Estate barriers, referred to earlier, were removed in the 1890s and Gower Street became the north-south race track it is now, that side of the Square was more or less cut off.

When the *London Review of Books* had not been long founded, in the early 1980s, I sent them a piece, speculatively, about the political shenanigans in Bermondsey where the Labour candidate, Peter Tatchell, was just about to be mauled in a notorious by-election, and where I also was involved as a party official. I was summoned to the then offices of the *LRB* on that east side of the Square to see the editor, Karl Miller, a rather austere figure who took out his fountain pen and ran through a short extra passage he had asked me to add on Tatchell himself. I sat quaking in my chair like a miscreant pupil in the headmaster's study until he finally grunted approval of some happy phrase, looked up, and indicated that the piece would appear. It was my first and last appearance in that paper whose offices today are in Little Russell Street, a few minutes' walk away.[1]

Countless writers have lived in Bedford Square. At No 1 the actor Weedon Grossmith lived in an Adams Brothers house and his brother George lived a short walk away in Russell Square. Together they wrote the *Diary of a Nobody*. At No 41 lived Anthony Hope who wrote *The Prisoner of Zenda* and A.J. Symonds at No 17, the poets Edward Fitzgerald at No 19 and Robert Bridges at No 52 and many more. At No 25, at the house of Basil Montagu, friend of Wordsworth and Coleridge, there were regular literary salons described by Thomas Carlyle in his *Reminiscences* in terms that make one think of the later Bloomsbury Group, as "a most singular social and spiritual menagerie; which, indeed, was well-known and much noted and criticised in certain literary and other circles". The scientist Henry Cavendish, who discovered hydrogen and the molecular composition of water, conducted all his experiments in his house at No 11 on the corner of Museum Place, not, as one might have supposed, the

Cavendish Laboratories at Cambridge.

But during the twentieth century Bedford Square ceased to be primarily residential and now mostly consists of offices: accountants, PR firms, Ed Victor's literary agency, and formerly, at No 30, publisher Jonathan Cape, up whose steps in the 1970s bounded Bruce Chatwin with the manuscript of *In Patagonia* in his rucksack. All along the western side stretches the Architectural Association, from No's 34 to 36. Founded in 1847 'the AA' has been in Bedford Square since 1920 and is the most prestigious architectural school in Britain, a private fee-paying institution wholly outside the public educational system. Its notable graduates include Zaha Hadid and Richard Rogers (not to mention Janet Street-Porter). In the summer, around party time, interesting architectural models suddenly appear on the pavements opposite, attracting puzzled looks from local office-workers and tourists.

In the centre of Bedford Square are the oval gardens, accessible only to those with a key as leaseholders, which means that it is a place to walk through rather than linger, a quiet refuge from the bustle of Tottenham Court Road. Another of those nineteenth century rhymesters, William Whitten, burst into song here:

Enough for me in yonder Square
To see the perky sparrows pair,
Or long laburnum gild the air
In Bloomsbury.

The birds are still here, though the "perky sparrows" have declined in number.

Imposing as all these stuccoed facades can be they say little about the interiors. What are these places like inside? Well, I should know, because for nearly three years in the late 1970s and early 1980s I worked here at No 26, at the National Council for Voluntary Organisations. Actually, I didn't work at No 26 but in one of its neighbours, but this is the pattern in so many of the Bloomsbury squares that have been turned over to office uses: judicious knocking-through creates long warrens of linked offices, whatever things might look like on the outside. Accordingly everyone visiting NCVO passed through the entrance at No 26, greeted at Reception by Dorothy with all the patrician charm she had acquired in the 1930s at Cheltenham Ladies College, and then moved through long passageways to the actual office they wanted. NCVO at that time had come under the leadership of the charismatic Nicholas Hinton, who later became head of Save the Children Fund until he died prematurely of a heart attack. Hinton was a remarkable boss, very well-connected socially with an exquisite little mews house in Victoria, to which certain staff were taken for working suppers, and who treated all of us with respect, especially those like me at the bottom of the hierarchy. There were still a few retired colonels and wing commanders who had 'gone into charity work' at NCVO but Hinton started to recruit lots of clever young graduates as part of a discreet modernisation of its image. Many of them went on to higher things, like Phil Hope, later MP for Luton, or my colleagues in the Information Department, Lindsey Williams, now head of Communications at the Wales Council for Voluntary Action in Mount Stuart Square, Cardiff, and Fiona MacTaggart, Labour MP for Slough and a former junior minister at the Home Office (herself, like Dorothy, a Cheltenham Ladies College graduate and a millionaire, her father, Sir Ian MacTaggart Bt, having been a multi-millionaire Glasgow property developer). I recall one Christmas lunch when we all crossed into Fitzrovia to an Italian restaurant and I threw out some mock-sexist quip of that facetious kind we Liverpudlians, alas, specialise in. Fiona missed the irony and a great, hard, shiny handbag came crashing down on my head. I can still feel it, thirty years on.

There were actually few internal architectural features that stick in my mind at No 26 and all I recall now are long, narrow corridors, rickety staircases and chipped white paint, but we were a lively bunch and it was a good place to work and I can see that it was here that my long love affair with Bloomsbury started to take permanent shape.

Our little platoon of walkers, having approved the architecture of the square, comes to a halt again opposite No 44, the home of Lady Ottoline Morrell. As an aristocrat, Lady Ottoline was probably a little higher in the social scale than the average Bloomsbury Group member, who tended to be more from the professional upper middle classes, but her fame and that of her salon have always been central to the idea of literary and artistic Bloomsbury. Striking – or strikingly ugly, depending on your point of view – Ottoline naturally found her way into fiction, in Aldous Huxley's *Crome Yellow* and D.H. Lawrence's *The Rainbow* (as Hermione) and was painted and written and gossiped about, often maliciously. She is an easy figure to mock but many of the most important British writers and artists of the early twentieth century passed through her hands and, as well as the snide gossip of Virginia Woolf and others, there were also generous tributes to her role as patron of the arts, a friend to the best, most innovative work of her day. "It is very difficult to think of anyone who meant so much to me," said T.S. Eliot simply. It was when, in 1906, her husband the Liberal MP Philip Morrell was elected to Parliament that she came to live in Bedford Square, staying until the purchase of the legendary old manor house in Oxfordshire, Garsington Manor in 1915. It was an open marriage on both sides and her lovers included Bertrand Russell and other Bloomsbury figures. Around 1907 her weekly parties at No 44 began and it was her intention at these gatherings to introduce rising young artists to rich patrons. Self-dramatising or controlling she may have been but she was also generous to artists and writers, providing opportunities and, at Garsington, refuge for so many. She was deeply hurt when she eventually learned from the painter Mark Gertler what people secretly thought of her, confessing to her private diary: "I am known as a dangerous and designing woman, immoral and unclean."[2] Not quite as rich as she seemed, financial difficulties led to the sale of Garsington in 1928 and her return with Philip to a more modest Bloomsbury house at No 10 Gower Street where they lived for the rest of their lives. She died in 1938.

GOWER STREET

The Morrell house in Gower Street is a few yards from Bedford Square and today, as noted above, it is not an attractive street to walk down because of the fast and noisy traffic. In 1891, Henry Wheatley, author of *London Past and Present,* wrote rather disparagingly of Gower Street that it was: "A dull, heavy street of commonplace houses, but as the leases fall in the houses are greatly improved, and in consequence the street wears a much brighter aspect."[3] Lord Eldon lived at No 42 from 1791-1804 and according to Wheatley: "he used to say that his house there was the pleasantest he ever occupied: he could look over the fields, then open, as far as Hampstead, Highgate, and Islington, and had a garden with excellent vegetables, and even peaches. Adjoining was a waste piece of ground; and 'men in London,' said he to Miss Foster, 'used to bring dogs to fight there, when I was Chief-Justice of the Common Pleas'." The actress Mrs Siddons bought a house in Gower St and wrote: "The back of it is most effectually in the country and delightfully pleasant." Today a vine grows up one of the Gower Street houses on the eastern side, the sole link with those peaches and rustic gardens open to the fields beyond.

Charles Darwin was another resident who appreciated this sylvan quality (so hard to imagine today) when he lived here from 1838 to 1842 in a house on the site of what is now the UCL Darwin building, 112 Gower Street, but was then 12 Upper Gower Street. Here he had his first two children and wrote his book on coral reefs. In a letter of October 1839 he wrote:

> We are living a life of extreme quietness... we have given up all parties, for they agree with neither of us; and if one is quiet in London there is nothing like its quietness; there is a grandeur about its smoky fogs and the dull distant sounds of cabs and coaches; in fact you may perceive I am becoming a thorough-paced cockney, and I glory in thoughts that I shall be here for the next six months.[4]

It was in Gower Street also that Mrs Micawber set up her brass plate (fruitlessly) to recruit young ladies in *David Copperfield.*

Gower Street began to be built in the 1780s and the uniformity of its plain brick houses, some of which later acquired bits and pieces of stucco, has never won it many friends. John Ruskin complained that it was "the *nec plus ultra* of ugliness in street architecture" and Pevsner says it was created "without much imagination". Part of the problem here is the University, whose role in the creation of the Bloomsbury townscape has seldom been uncontroversial.

LONDON UNIVERSITY

The traditional sparring between Grub Street and Academe, which used to have freelance scribblers like myself tilting at the tenured occupants of Varsity chairs, and involves the latter fighting back by dismissing our efforts as mere journalese and hack-work, has for some time now ceased to be an affordable luxury. Both sides realise that they need each other in these days of dwindling readerships for serious books and hectic dumbing-down in the publishing trade. So, as I stroll through the University district I am on my best behaviour. No sniping please.

The real difficulty with universities today, of course, is their widespread adoption of a business ethic and the way in which government funding is proposed to be tied to the notorious 'impact'

criterion which rewards only research which has a visible monetary outcome. As the narrator of a recent J.M. Coetzee novel puts it, the function of universities today is to make money, and rather a lot of vice-chancellors are more than happy with this. In particular the self-appointed 'Russell Group' of 'top' universities (so-called because they used to meet as a caucus in the Russell Hotel in Russell Square, before going on to the official meeting of the Committee of Vice-Chancellors and Principals in Tavistock Square) have made clear that they are itching to be allowed to raise their student tuition fees still higher. In the words of the director-general of the Russell Group: "The most effective and efficient way of protecting the quality of UK higher education would be to allow institutions to exercise discretion over the level of graduate contributions they require." Translated into plain English this means: "We want to put the prices up." The Russell Group wants the cap on student tuition fees removed altogether so that universities can charge as much as they want, which could result in many students, according to the National Union of Students, leaving university with debts of over £40,000. For all these reasons marketing slogans have become obligatory in higher education and sure enough, here stuck to the street signs half way up Gower Street is the new slogan adopted by University College: 'London's global university'. I often pause to reflect on this phrase. Unlike Birkbeck's 'London's evening university', which makes sense, I have not the slightest idea what 'London's global university' means. But that is probably the point of marketing slogans, they aren't really meant to mean anything, just create a vague sort of para-semantic buzz. And when it comes to marketing, University College London (or 'UCL') is the champion, selling its brand with unerring success and confounding the expectations of its early critics.

London University first opened its doors in 1828 to provide education for the sort of people for whom Oxford and Cambridge was not an option. At that time, unless you were a professing

Christian, happy to subscribe to the Thirty-Nine Articles of the Christian faith, the ancient universities were out of bounds. But there was more to it than this. The rising nineteenth century middle class wanted its own institutions, based on its material values. One of the intellectual inspirers of the new London University was the poet Thomas Campbell who dreamed of "a great London university" for "the youth of our middling rich people".[5] The utilitarian philosopher Jeremy Bentham, whose clothed skeleton – the famous 'auto-icon' – is displayed in its box in the UCL South Cloisters, denounced Oxford and Cambridge as "the two great nuisances" and "storehouses and nurseries of political corruption". Rising London businessmen liked the idea of putting their sons into a London university modelled to some extent on the Universities of Bonn, or Virginia or Edinburgh and since nonconformists and Jews were still barred from Oxbridge there was good reason to launch a university in the capital. The Deed of Settlement signed on February 11th 1826 declared that the "object of the said Institution is the advancement of literature and science by affording to young men residing or resorting to the Cities of London and Westminster, the Borough of Southwark, and Counties adjoining to either of the said Cities, or to the said Borough, adequate opportunities for acquiring literary and scientific education at a moderate expense."

The Establishment, of course, fought back and the new University was mocked as 'The Cockney College'. The poet Winthrop Mackworth Praed wrote a spoof 'Discourse' delivered by a port-soaked Oxford college tutor to his peers in 1825 when the new University was being mooted:

Ye Dons and ye Doctors, ye Provosts and Proctors,
Who are paid to monopolize knowledge,
Come, make opposition, by vote and petition,
To the radical infidel college...

But let them not babble of Greek to the rabble,
Nor teach the Mechanics their letters;
The labouring classes were born to be asses,
And not to be aping their betters.[6]

The poem cleverly exposed the snobbish fear that the proposed London University would allow the lower orders into the sanctified world of learning. The Oxbridge dons in the poem are alarmed that "fat butchers" and "looking-glass makers" – *tradesmen* in short – might be sending their sons (women's education still lagged behind and it was 1868 before the London Ladies Educational Association was founded to provide classes for women and 1878 before women were admitted on the same footing as men) to learn medicine and philosophy. What is more, they would be nonconformists or even atheists ("sabbath-breakers") and the lumpenproletariat would be forsaking its usual pastimes for the seminar room ("The gin-shops are turn'd into cloisters"). To many of the readers of *The Morning Chronicle* in which this poem first appeared on 19th July 1825, this was an unbearable thought. They need not have fretted, because today, UCL is one of the most élitist parts of the British higher education system: a third of its places going to students from private fee-paying schools, one of the highest proportions of any British university. Less than one undergraduate in five has a working-class background. The Cockney rabble has been seen off.

Back in 1825 the promoters of the new University between them bought eight acres of land for £30,000 on a site previously used as a drilling ground, a duelling space, and a rubbish dump. Once earmarked for the creation of yet another square which would have been known as Carmarthen Square (and also used in 1808 to show off Trevethick's experimental passenger railway), the university site was acquired and the architect William Wilkins came up with a fashionable neo-Grecian design, sniffily dismissed by Pugin as pagan: "in character with the intentions and principles of the institution". Greek Revival architecture was clearly being associated with nonconformist culture. The Establishment lost no time in launching plans for an anti-UCL in the shape of King's College and a meeting was addressed by Rev. Dr George D'Oyly, the Rector of Lambeth in June 1928 chaired by the Duke of Westminster – prompted by the shocking news of the exclusion of religious teaching from a University in the heart of London. King's College opened in October 1831.

The University of London obtained its first charter in 1836 and changed its name in that year to University College London. Wilkins' Grecian original can be seen from the north end of Gower Street by passing through the main gates into the campus. Its huge portico of ten columns was modelled on the Temple of Jupiter Olympus at Athens. Today's University of London is the overall degree-awarding body, and it covers UCL and King's and over time has acquired many other colleges and institutions, such as Birkbeck, founded as

the London Mechanics' Institute in 1824. This expansion led to its acquiring more land in Bloomsbury from 1927 onwards and to growing controversy about its destruction of Bloomsbury's Georgian squares. This reached a peak in 1969 when the University pressed for more of Woburn Square's Georgian buildings to be demolished, claiming that the property had been acquired in 1927 and planning permission acquired as long ago as 1932 (when no one bothered much about the preservation of Georgian architecture). As Hermione Hobhouse argues in *Lost London* the London County Council planners were helpless: "It is therefore London University and its architects that must bear the responsibility for deciding to destroy Gordon Square and its ancillary streets, Gordon and Taviton Streets, parts of Gower Street, the west side of Russell Square and, finally, both Torrington and Woburn Squares, either of which could have provided an almost collegiate heart to the precinct, had this been what the University and its architects wanted."[7]

The consequence of all this for the ordinary Bloomsbury *flâneur* is that a substantial segment of Bloomsbury is covered by large university buildings some of which, like Nicholas Hare's 1995 Brunei Gallery and School of Oriental and African Studies extension, are exciting and attractive buildings – especially the gallery and the oriental garden on the roof. Other buildings, like so many of the halls of residence, are dire, but amongst them one can pick one's way and find shortcuts and spaces to sit on hot summer days. A particularly nice stroll I often make is out of Russell Square's north west corner by the Faber Building, along the backside of Denys Lasdun's massive Institute of Advanced Legal Studies and Institute of Education, towards what is left of Woburn Square, still a nice, tranquil spot of greenery even if only one row of Georgian houses is left on the eastern side. Beyond it is Gordon Square, larger and greener still.

And everywhere there are students. What is Bloomsbury like for them? There is only one way to find out. I decided to ask a postgraduate, living in a student house in one of those attractive remaining

Georgian buildings, to join me in the coffee bar in the basement of the University Bookshop in Gower Street and explain what it is like to live and work as a student in Bloomsbury. Rachael Bedford, daughter of the poet William Bedford, is researching her psychology doctorate. Her first impressions after arriving from Oxford were of a "maze-like" complex of squares and colleges that could be initially confusing to pick one's way through but where everything was on the spot: "It feels like a complete area in itself." She explains that student life revolves around bars and coffee bars inside each college which the rest of us, without our security bleepers, simply don't know about. But it changes character in the evening when those who live as well as work on the site see staff and students lodging in the suburbs disappear: "It feels like quite a different place in the evening." For those who are here all the time, with libraries open all day and night every day of the week, it's an intense experience: "It's got everything that I want but it's hard to get closure on what you're doing." The city never sleeps either and all the facilities of a major capital are within immediate reach. Being a student is a temporary phase, which intensifies the experience: "There's a sense of wanting to make the most of a year." And in shared student housing in the heart of Bloomsbury there is: "A pressure to get to know people straightaway." So many nationalities thrown together, so many birds of passage: "In a sense it is a strange way to live."

IN SEARCH OF THE AUTO-ICON

It is time to visit the University College campus to search out that famous 'auto-icon' of Jeremy Bentham, UCL's spiritual father – even though he wasn't practically involved in setting up the University as is often claimed. No one challenges me as I wander about the Wilkins building looking for the philosopher. I first head for the Bentham Room which turns out to be a mistake because it seems to be a canteen whose Central European staff have never heard of my man. I carry on along the spacious corridors until I spot someone wearing an official badge who turns out to be an examination invigilator. A pleasant elderly Irish woman, she tries to whip me into the examination hall, thinking I am a latecomer but I explain my mission. She gestures in the right direction: "Ach! He must be some kind of fellow who had one enormous ego by the look of him. Sitting there." Madam, this is no way to speak of our philanthropic betters. And,

sure enough, round the next corner, there he is, in a polished wooden box with open glass doors (do they shut them up at night like the door of a hen house?) in a frock coat, silk scarf, and broad-brimmed straw hat. His little house reminds me of one of those elaborate confessional boxes in an Italian cathedral. It has his name in gilt letters on the pediment. It's not quite as grisly as it sounds because this is not the mummified body, rather a clothed skeleton, and the head is a waxwork, the real one kept in a university safe. But she was right, it does take a bit of *chutzpah* to leave an instruction in your will that your skeleton be exhibited for the edification of the populace, particularly when your sayings include: "All inequality is a source of evil" or "every individual in the country tells for one; no individual more than one". The whole thing, of course, could just be a kind of joke, as indeed some think it is. But in his will he left instructions which included the passage: "If it should so happen that my personal friends and other disciples should be disposed to meet together on some day or days of the year for the purpose of commemorating the founder of the greatest happiness system of morals and legislation my executor will from time to time cause to be conveyed to the room in which they meet the said box or case with the contents therein to be stationed in such part of the room as to the assembled company shall seem meet." This sounds rather like the annual display of a saint's relic on his or her feast day at a religious procession in the heart of Catholic Europe, but then Bentham is a sort of rationalist saint to his 'disciples'.

UCL is obviously proud of its venerated holy man and the little shrine in an open corridor has an historical display about his life and work and various free leaflets are available. One of Bentham's big ideas was the Panopticon. It was actually invented by his brother, Samuel, a naval architect who was working for Prince Potemkin in Russia in the 1780s and who came up with the idea of the "all-seeing place" where workers could be monitored constantly by the boss. His brother was very excited by this notion of "a new mode of obtaining power of mind over mind". He would have been thrilled by today's surveillance society with CCTV cameras at every turn. Jeremy Bentham immediately saw the wider applications of the Panopticon, especially for prisons. He believed that people behaved better if they were being spied upon. He also wanted prisons to be run by the private sector because, in good utilitarian style, the promise of profit would unite the contractor's duty with his self-interest. He never built his prison nor did he build his panopticon 'industry-houses' where the poor would be forced to work for relief whilst being permanently monitored. Some of his ideas were later enshrined in the New Poor Law of 1834. Michel Foucault saw the panopticon as the paradigm of the modern state, but Bentham's defenders say that his ideal society worked the other way round, with citizens watching their rulers through fully open and accountable government. It all sounds to me too close to what we now have in twenty-first century Britain: a society of too many spy-cameras, email monitoring, police photographing of legitimate demonstrators, and creeping (and creepy) extensions of the security state, as well as workplaces where the bosses keep people under close watch, replacing creative management and inspired leadership with petty punitive surveillance, sugar-coated with a kind of Google-geek spurious equality, and with everyone, as Aldous Huxley warned in *Brave New World,* loving every minute of their voluntary slavery. Personally I would put the genius of Bentham back in its box.

TORRINGTON PLACE AND 'DILLON'S'

The University bookshop is currently run by the Waterstone's chain but for many of us it will always be 'Dillon's'. The original proprietor, Una Dillon, started out in Store Street, and the only thing that seems to have changed apart from the owner's name, is the presence outside of fairly insistent women in headscarves selling copies of the *Big Issue.* If the architecture is reminiscent of the ornate splendour of the Russell Hotel that's because it was designed by the same architect, Charles Fitzroy Doll, and the high gables and excess of terracotta ornament contrast with the prevailing dullness of most of the University buildings which surround it. The Department of National Heritage refers to its "elaborate Franco-Flemish-Gothic style" which seems good enough for me. Pevsner calls it "a wild block" and maybe a little wildness is what is needed here to counter the institutional drabness and functionalism. The main entrance opens onto

Torrington Place, facing the newest UCL buildings and, down a side alley on that side of the street is the Petrie Museum of Egyptian Archaeology, a curiously old-fashioned place (though there are plans in hand for a major revamp in 2011) which is reminiscent of an unmodernised museum in provincial Greece with its typed or handwritten cards and jumble of dusty bits and pieces. At the reception desk a kindly elderly woman offers me a torch to help see those display cases that are in subdued lighting. It is more of a teaching resource at present than a twenty-first century museum – with all the gimmicks and directive curatorial information panels that would imply. The Department of Egyptian Archaeology and Philology at UCL and the Museum are the result of a bequest in 1892 by the Victorian writer, traveller, and pioneer Egyptologist, Amelia Edwards, of her personal collection. This was supplemented by material from the excavations of William Flinders Petrie, the famous archaeological digger, who sold his collection to UCL in 1915 when the museum was opened (though not to the general public at first). Since export of antiquities from Egypt and the Sudan is now illegal the collection of 80,000 objects, including the inevitable mummy, has stopped growing.

The University Bookshop on its northern sides fronts Gower Street and on its southern flank is Malet Street where there is yet another trades union building. Dilke House, a 1930s block houses the London regional offices of the Union of Shop, Distributive and Allied Workers, and a little further down the street, the Vanbrugh Theatre and bar of the Royal Academy of Dramatic Art (RADA) whence everyone from Kenneth Branagh to Diana Rigg seems to have graduated. But any sort of 'theatrical' flamboyance is not in evidence in the wide, empty space of Malet Street. On the opposite side the students union building and Birkbeck College rear entrance give way to Senate House at the southern end. This tall, grey sort-of-art-deco building of Portland Stone (see p.146), designed in 1937 by Charles Holden (more celebrated for his London Underground stations) gave Orwell the idea of the Ministry of Truth, because he worked there during the war for the Ministry of Information alongside Dylan Thomas and others. It was second in height only to St Paul's in London when it was built. It was eventually used in the film version of *Nineteen Eighty Four* and remains a popular location for film-makers, from the creators of Batman movies to period thrillers. It is often ringed by refreshment caravans and buses and film vans when the latest shoot is on. Senate House is one of those buildings that are rather more interesting inside than out and I like its Travertine marble floors and fancy bronze internal railings and doorways. It also houses the University Library.

Malet Street ends at Montague Place and the north entrance to the British Museum outside which, day in and day out, a battered little mobile African Canteen serves exotic food and hot drinks to the weary museum-bibbers while the bored drivers of parked tourist coaches catch up on some kip.

The University Bookshop opens out to the northeast into Byng Place, beyond which is Gordon Square. There is a nice early nineteenth century building there by Thomas Cubitt, the architect of so much in Bloomsbury, whose houses in Woburn Square across the way fell to the bulldozers in the 1960s; this was originally Coward College, which trained dissenting Protestant ministers. It was until quite recently a cheap hostel run by the International Centre for the Society of Friends that friends of mine used to stay in, but is now part of the university residential resources. Behind it is the great Gothic mass of the University Church of Christ the King. This looming Bath stone monster is nearly always shut and there are menacing warnings about not taking photographs inside should it ever be open. The smaller chapel fronting Gordon Street, however, is open on weekdays and is a calm and reflective space. John Betjeman liked Christ the King and called it "without a doubt, the grandest church in London of the pioneer days of the Gothic Revival". It was built in 1853 for an eccentric sect called the Catholic Apostolic Church, or the Irvingites.

Edward Irving was a Scottish Presbyterian (who also preached at the 'Scotch Church' in Regent Square) who founded his sect in the 1820s and practised a form of ritualist nonconformism under the direction of a college of 'apostles' who claimed to possess the gift of tongues. A friend of Thomas Carlyle, Irving preached the imminent end of the world – but Babylon has survived him. In place of the bishop's throne was the "Angel's throne" and various Catholic Apostolic features like the seven hanging lamps hung before the altar. The sect eventually withered away and the building became the university church in 1963.

Today's Cloisters are now let as flats and next door is Dr William's Library, a special library of nonconformist literature, which took up residence here in 1890 (Queen Square was an earlier Bloomsbury resting place for the library) after the occupants of what was University Hall moved out to Manchester. University Hall is famous for having had as its first principal in 1849, the poet Arthur Hugh Clough, who, having been unable to subscribe at Oxford to the Thirty Nine Articles, sampled the Unitarianism of University Hall, which was set up to house Unitarian students at UCL in the wake of the religious freedoms permitted by the Dissenting Chapels Act. But Clough seems to have found Unitarianism no more appealing than Oxford Anglican orthodoxy and he soon moved on.

UCL's 'Bloomsbury Project' which aims to catalogue the history of nineteenth century reforming institutions – what I have unkindly called Worthy Bloomsbury – has unearthed no fewer than 62 educational establishments in the area, between 1800 and 1904 according to its 'Bloomsbury Blog', and to these can be added the learned societies, organisations for ministering to the poor and the lower classes, hospitals and charities that the Project plans to document. This side of Bloomsbury can sometimes lead one to yearn for a little more vivacity and colour, something *louche* or wild, but one will hope in vain for this in the precincts of Gower Street.

It is time for me to plunge into Tottenham Court Road again.

TOTTENHAM COURT ROAD

At the south-western corner of Bloomsbury, where New Oxford Street meets Tottenham Court Road, the jostling crowds pause before plunging west into the maelstrom of Oxford Street, under the eye of Centre Point. Swarms of shoppers, tourists, office workers and

people out for a good time in the West End pour like disturbed ants out of Tottenham Court Road Underground station, and around the Tube entrance vendors of dodgy looking 'designer' watches try to solicit trade while touts from the language schools hand out their printed cards for courses in English. The pavements are dirty and littered. You jostle for space. This is not Woburn Square gardens.

Leaving behind the Dominion Theatre (which has been showing the rock musical *I Will Rock You* for simply *ages*) I move northwards along the Road past the hi-fi shops which are still here though outnumbered now by computer retailers. I still possess (thanks to the skill of a repair man operating out of a garden shed in rural Powys) a Trio stereo amplifier bought here in 1980, its sound as sweet as ever, but Tottenham Court Road's southern end is today the province of the serious new technology shopper. Some of these businesses, selling laptops and cameras and mobile phones and gadgetry, are more like North African souks than conventional retail outlets and you often have to haggle over unpriced items. Whether there are genuine bargains to be had I can't decide. Internet sites are probably a better option for much of this electronic hardware. Tottenham Court Road, fortunately, gets more interesting the further away from the Underground I go north. Opposite Goodge Street Underground (which marks the boundary, for me, of Bloomsbury and Fitzrovia whose streets begin here west of Tottenham Court Road) is Heal's furniture store, on the eastern side at No 196, the most striking building in the whole street.

HEAL'S AND HABITAT

Tottenham Court Road in its northern reaches is the home of furniture stores and, especially, bed makers. I sleep, at Strachey Mansions, on a very comfortable sofa bed from Highly Sprung, one of many bedmakers still trading. They all came here originally from Camden Town to the north which was once the centre of piano manufacture. When this trade declined their carpentry skills found an obvious outlet in bed manufacture but Heals, with its 1917 facade of decorative cast-iron panels representing the various kinds of furniture manufacture, is the star turn. Sir Ambrose Heal, the most famous of the Heals, was born in 1872 into the family bedding business that had been founded in 1810 by his great-grandfather. The site was right on top of Capper's Farm and the firm's bedding factory was built on the old cowsheds. During the building of another extension many animal bones were found. The fields beneath.

Ambrose Heal had studied at the Slade School of Art and he had more ambitious plans as a furniture maker than any hitherto seen by the firm. He started to design simple sturdy pieces of furniture made out of oak which were dubbed by his more conventional staff 'prison furniture'. He was no doubt determined to counter the snobbery of the arts and crafts movement about Tottenham Court Road furniture styles and today Heal's, and its neighbour, Habitat, still reflect this plain modern style, even when the latter's stylish exteriors mask chipboard with veneer.

Ambrose Heal was a founding member of the Design and Industries Association, set up in 1914 by various designers and manufacturers who wanted to emulate the German pre-War record of infusing industrial production with arts-and-crafts values. Their catchphrase 'good design' embodied an idea of good workmanship and fitness for purpose that is still found in Heal's furniture today. Ambrose personally designed the Heal's distinctive four-poster bed logo, commissioned one of the most distinctive shop buildings in London, and opened an art gallery on the top of the building that exhibited work by Picasso, Wyndham Lewis, and Modigliani. Sir Hugh Casson said that in the 1930s "Heal's was a symbol rather than a shop." It was a bit like Terence Conran's later invention, Habitat, whose shop is next door. Ambrose Heal was also a friend of the designer Gordon

Russell, another twentieth century design pioneer and his son, Anthony, served an apprenticeship at Gordon Russell's furniture workshops in Broadway, Worcestershire, working in the same tradition until changes in fashion and the marketplace led to Heal's being sold in 1983 to Conran's Habitat-Mothercare group.

At around the same time as Ambrose Heal was bringing about his revolution in the furniture trade, a more highbrow design experiment was taking place a few hundred yards away at 33 Fitzroy Square where in July 1913 the Omega Workshops opened to the public, with Bloomsbury artists Vanessa Bell, Duncan Grant and Roger Fry as directors. Roger Fry was the presiding genius and his ambition was to end what he saw as a false dichotomy between the fine and the decorative arts (rather than being concerned with the social values and critique of industrialism that the William Morris-inspired arts and crafts movement emphasised in their practice). Post-Impressionism was the flavour of the month for forward-looking artists and Fry and Omega tried to apply to design some of that movement's bright colours and bold, simplified forms. Popular newspapers like the *Daily News*, responded by calling the Omega products in one headline: POST-IMPRESSIONIST FURNITURE. The polemical artist and writer Wyndham Lewis, an early collaborator in the Omega project, soon fell out (characteristically) with Fry over his handling of a commission for the 1913 Ideal Home Exhibition, where Omega and Heal's, would have rubbed shoulders and went off to found the Rebel Art Centre.

"Couples were drawn into the shop, magnetised by the artificial homeliness they were searching for. Now, for a second their vision was clear and unimpaired – so this is what a home is like – our home – as if a glimpse of eternity had been revealed to them, then quickly wiped away," wrote Isobel English in her 1956 novel, *Every Eye*, capturing the aspiration of countless Habitat and Heal's customers right up to the present day.

After Heal's and Habitat, Tottenham Court Road loses itself in more shops. On the corner of University Street (which follows the lines of one of the openings of the eighteenth century fields and was originally known as Carmarthen Street) is an art deco block of flats called Paramount Court, which readers of the novelist Jenny Diski will be familiar with as she has often written about her childhood there in books like *Skating to Antarctica*. Also in University Street is a pub once known as 'the Welly Bar' (Lord Wellington) by its medical student clientele, but renamed the Jeremy Bentham in 1982 to

commemorate the 150th anniversary of the death of the philosopher.

At the junction of Torrington Place and Tottenham Court Road is Habitat, where the shop assistants are what they have always been since I remember coming to London: black-clad and *chic*, matching the young customers who come in search of affordable passing styles – I still wince at those once ultra-trendy chocolate brown coffee mugs from the late 1970s, two of which are still left in the cupboard! Torrington Place is dominated by large, solid, mansion blocks which I have always found intriguing, more Parisian than English in their ornate anonymity behind heavy doors. Turning right shortly after the cavernously Victorian Marlborough Arms pub at No 36 into Ridgmount Street there's a blue plaque celebrating the (rather brief!) residence in one of these solid mansion blocks, in the 1960s of the singer Bob Marley. Built in the 1880s, these flats were intended to be for "other than the artisan or labouring classes", a rule that one can feel fully confident is still being observed. At the end of Ridgmount Street, where it meets Store Street, is a very sad sight. Until only a year or so ago, and still partly visible behind the hoardings, was an exquisite little eggshell blue Art Deco petrol filling station, the oldest operational filling station in central London, trading since 1926. It was originally the Duke of Bedford's private garage. I can imagine Mr Toad getting out of his open car here and waiting, in exquisitely tooled leather gloves, his goggles up on his forehead, for his tank to be filled. Less glamorous petrol stations like that attached to Strachey Mansions have also gone after the introduction of the congestion charge to limit car traffic in central London dealt a death-blow to the petrol trade. I fully approve of the charge as a means of improving the quality of life and the efficiency of public transport but I also shed a tear for Bloomsbury Service Station, R.I.P.

STORE STREET

Store Street itself, a pleasant, leafy, tolerably quiet street, that was in the early eighteenth century part of a nine-acre field known as Cantelowes Close, also has an Art Deco flavour – as the Deco Café opposite at this Gower Street end reminds me. A civilised café patronised by University staff (I have more than once caught sight of the silver-maned philosopher A.C. Grayling in Socratic dialogue with a colleague or two in there) it has chairs outside under the canvas awning giving a slightly continental flavour to the street, picked up by some Italian cafés, also with outdoor tables, though these properties are all currently being refurbished by the Bedford Estate. The tiny University Tavern, servicing the students at the College of Law next door has re-christened itself, presumably to curry favour with the trainee lawyers, the College Arms but its charms continue to elude me. On its other side at No 16 there was once a music hall but that would seem too boisterous for today's deco-decorous street. Recessed at the Tottenham Court Road end, South Crescent contains the headquarters of the Building Centre which was originally built after the First World War as a Daimler showroom and the splendidly titled Imagination House which turns out to be a design and communications consultancy whose re-modelled interior won it the accolade of Royal Fine Arts Commission 'building of the year' in 1989. From here, a short walk north along Alfred Place into Chenies Street brings me to one of the oddest-looking buildings in Bloomsbury, a pink and white structure that looks like a half-demolished Tube station, behind a war memorial. It is called The Eisenhower Centre, and it completely ruins the North Crescent that should balance the South Crescent behind me in Store Street. It turns out to be the entrance to an underground network of tunnels started in 1941, the year, incidentally, that a bomb destroyed, with heavy loss of life, a Jewish girls' club in Alfred Place and the West Central synagogue next door. It was one of eight deep shelters in central London for

the Important People rather than the general public during the war which were mostly used as communications centres. At the end of 1942 General Eisenhower was given the whole underground complex at Goodge Street to use as the signals centre for the Supreme HQ Allied Expeditionary Force and much of the planning for the D-Day landings was completed here. After the war the Chenies Street building was an army transit station and later, after a major fire in 1956, it ended up as a security archive.

Mention of the West Central synagogue's destruction by wartime bombing recalls that there are several other centres of Jewish culture in Bloomsbury that seem to have vanished. Opposite the British Medical Association in Tavistock Square, for example, used to be the Jews' College, with a first floor museum. This is the ancestor of today's London School of Jewish Studies in Hendon. It was founded by Chief Rabbi Nathan Adler and opened on 11 November 1855. The College has always had very close links with the Chief Rabbinate, as many Jewish leaders, including Lord Jakobovits and Sir Israel Brodie have graduated from the institution. The College was proposed on 4 January 1852 at a public meeting chaired by Sir Moses Montefiore who was the head of the Sephardic community in England and the generally recognised head of the Anglo-Jewish community. When the College opened three years later with 33 pupils it was "for the purpose of affording a liberal and useful Hebrew and English education to the sons of respectable parents, and training of ministers, readers and teachers," combining a Jewish day school and a ministerial training college. Jews' College was first located at fashionable 10 Finsbury Square, where many prosperous London Jews lived. Since then it has moved five times. In 1881 it moved to Tavistock House where Dickens lived, then in 1900 to Queen Square, then Woburn House in Upper Woburn Place, Montague Place in 1957, and finally leaving Bloomsbury in 1984, the year in which it moved to its current location in Hendon. The Jews' College Library is said to be one of the best libraries of Jewish material in Europe.

Back in Chenies Street, the Drill Hall Arts Centre has been since 1975 a leading arts venue. The building originally opened in 1882 as a drill hall for the Bloomsbury Rifles but was also used in the early twentieth century as a rehearsal space for Diaghilev's legendary Ballets Russes and Nijinsky. During the Second World War it was used as a similar rehearsal space for Ralph Reader's gang shows. Today, the Centre says it is "led and illuminated by a gay, lesbian and queer aesthetic"; it has a reputation for bold and innovative productions.

GORDON SQUARE AND WOBURN SQUARE AND (AT LAST) THE BLOOMSBURY GROUP

Some pages ago I left my Blue Badge Guide and his group of overseas visitors in Bedford Square. The party eventually moved off and, via some important diversions at places I have already talked about, ended up in Gordon Square, coming to a halt outside a tall, stuccoed building, facing the leafy square on its eastern side. No 46 Gordon Square is the centre or *omphalos* of that curious and unignorable phenomenon 'Bloomsbury' and I have left this until the end because it might well have overwhelmed and consumed this little book given the Group's voracious appetite for gossip and anecdote. For, more than anything else, the word 'Bloomsbury' still means for most people in Britain and around the world that constellation of literary, artistic and intellectual talent that came together early in the twentieth century in what was by then the relatively unfashionable London district of Bloomsbury and whose leading names were Virginia Woolf, Lytton Strachey, Maynard Keynes, Clive and Vanessa Bell, Leonard Woolf, Roger Fry, Duncan Grant – with E.M. Forster, Bertrand Russell, Ottoline Morell and many others swelling the scene. The Bloomsbury Group or Bloomsbury Set (as a hairdressing salon in Bloomsbury Street calls itself) arouses strong emotions and everyone has an opinion about them – even now.

But first, Gordon Square. In the centre is an especially beautiful garden, which compensates Gordon Square for the former ravages of the varsity bulldozers between it and Woburn Square to the west. Camden Council, which has been doing such outstanding work in the last few years in improving the Bloomsbury Squares, has done a particularly good job with Gordon Square. They have defied the old ideas about municipal parks that I remember from my childhood, which ordained that public gardens were savagely policed by mowers, and clippers and edgers, with regimented flowerbeds and not a leaf out of place. In the spring Gordon Square is a delight, with patches of wild spring flowers – bluebells and primroses and forget-me-nots – allowed to grow freely. It's popular, unsurprisingly, with students who spread themselves out on the grass and is yet another peaceful, civilised space in the heart of London. It's hard to imagine that it was on this site, as the author of the *Curiosities of London* puts it, that: "a circular enclosure was constructed, about the year 1803, for the exhibition of the first locomotive, the production of Trevithick.... Its performance was then so satisfactory that a bet was offered by the proprietors to match the engine to run a greater number of miles in twenty-four hours than any horse that could be produced. But there were no takers!"[9]

Gordon Square, named after Lady Georgiana Gordon, second wife of the sixth Duke of Bedford, who personally supervised the layout of the gardens, was actually developed later than the other Bloomsbury Squares. Some of the houses started by Thomas Cubitt, who left his mark on so many of the squares after he took over from James Burton as the principal architect-developer in 1820, were finished in the 1850s by his successors and are looked on rather sniffily by architectural historians. By this time Bloomsbury was becoming unfashionable and the Bedford Estate and Cubitt struggled to compete with Belgravia or Hyde Park Gate which were considered more smart and stylish districts. The fledgling University was, in these circumstances, a welcome client. Originally, Woburn Square and Gordon Square were marshy ground, on which development was considered the best thing, but the houses built in Woburn Square to the south were of lower quality than the Bloomsbury norm. The University bought the squares from the Bedford Estate in 1951 and it was in the 1950s that the Warburg Institute (which used to house the marvellous collection of paintings, one of my favourites in London, that is now in the Courtauld Institute Galleries in Somerset House in the Strand) was built by Charles Holden, the famous Underground station architect. In the late 1960s a row of nine terraced houses on the eastern side of Woburn Square was demolished to create the building site for the massive Institute of Education and then in 1972 the southern section of Woburn Square gardens was lopped off to enable the School of Oriental and African Studies extension, also by Denys Lasdun, to be built. Originally Woburn Square would have stretched as far south as Russell Square but what is left is certainly one of Bloomsbury's most tranquil

garden squares, long and narrow, with a small wooden shelter with seats at the northern end. At the southern end Lydia Kapinska's 1999 bronze statue of 'The Green Man' rears from a flower bed to illustrate a passage from Virginia Woolf's *The Waves*. ("My roots go down to the depths of the world, through earth dry brick, and damp earth, through veins of lead and silver. I am all fibre.").

46 Gordon Square was later occupied, in 1916, by John Maynard Keynes, who married in 1925 the Russian Lydia Lopokova, a prima ballerina in the Diaghilev company. In 1948 she moved to Cambridge, but her housekeeper still lived in the basement flat as late as the early 1970s. When Keynes died in 1946, the University acquired the house and several others in the eastern row and radically altered the interiors to house the new Institute for Computer Studies at 42-47. It now houses the History of Art Department. From 1909-1924 Lytton Strachey lived at No 51 and his brother James, translator of Freud, lived at No 41 from 1919-1956.

Back outside No 46, the guide's quip about the Bloomsbury Group "moving in circles and loving in triangles" captures the public perception of a highly privileged and elite group whose private lives as much as their ideas were designed to affront conventional mores.

We need to get to the bottom of this.

BLOOMSBURY

In her indispensable and witty guide to the whole 'Bloomsbury' phenomenon, *Bloomsbury Pie: The Story of the Bloomsbury Revival* (1997) Regina Marler concludes: "But make no mistake: 'Bloomsbury' remains a dirty word. In fact, it may be more culturally useful as a term of abuse than as a neutral adjective or proper noun."[10] This ought to strike us rather oddly but somehow it doesn't. Why would a group of extremely talented writers, artists and thinkers attract such opprobrium? Shouldn't we rather be celebrating and enjoying the products of their talent? Although the puritanical critic F.R. Leavis sniffed that Bloomsbury was "a very inferior social milieu" (most people would argue that the problem was that, actually, it wasn't) a dispassionate outsider would surely see: one of a handful of great and innovative early twentieth century English novelists, Virginia Woolf, a great economist, John Maynard Keynes, a revolutionary biographer, Lytton Strachey, who turned a moribund genre on its head and revivified it, several artists and art critics of distinction, a philosopher or two, and ask why they should be the object of mockery or even contempt. Even allowing for the vigorous populist strain in English culture that despises 'intellectuals' and 'arty' people, and which means that the running commentary on a Thames tourist boat (in contrast to a New York cruise around Manhattan) will automatically assume that, as it passes Tate Modern, visitors will want to hear sneering gibes about 'modern art', why does Bloomsbury rattle so many people?

Perhaps the real answer lies in the fact that Bloomsbury never gave a thought to its image, assuming that its privileged metropolitan milieu was sufficient to itself. The arrogance was hard-wired, the battle-lines of English class and culture firmly drawn up, the social assurance (notwithstanding the cataclysm of the First World War that started to break out around it) seemingly intact. But if Bloomsbury and its cast list were so awful, why the fascination? Why is the National Portrait Gallery's postcard of Virginia Woolf, which Regina Marler calls "the corporate logo of Bloomsbury", one of its best-selling cards? Why do the memoirs of very minor characters in the Bloomsbury soap opera still get read and talked about? The answer is probably not very edifying and has something to do with the English obsession with class and social snobbery, the love-hate relationship with People Who Are Not Like Us.

One result of this ambivalence is that even the members of the Bloomsbury Group itself, in spite of being regularly accused of being too superior by half, were queerly defensive when they tried to explain themselves. The revival of interest in Bloomsbury in the 1960s (at least in part to do with the rediscovery of the artists and the skilful work of certain dealers in raising their stock) was marked by a number of autobiographical accounts by some of those centrally involved. One of their most constant themes was that they were not really a group at all, merely a loose association of like-minded friends, who had been branded and classified largely by other people. Sometimes there was a certain weary languor about these protestations that makes one wonder about the extent to which such rebuttals were disingenuous.

Leonard Woolf, one of the most attractive of the Bloomsbury memorialists, whose four volumes of autobiography tell us a great deal of what we want to know about the group, insists that what came to be called Bloomsbury by the others "never existed in the form given to it by the outside world. For 'Bloomsbury' was and is currently used as a term – usually of abuse – applied to a largely imaginary group of persons with largely imaginary objects and characteristics".[11] This theme is repeated by many of the principal actors in the Bloomsbury story and amounts to a claim that, although it might look to everyone else like a closed little clique, that is not how they saw it. But the evidence to the contrary is overwhelming. Not merely did the same people constantly come together, in often quite formal ways, they shared certain strongly defined social values, intellectual characteristics, aesthetic and moral values, that were explicit and much-discussed – the importance set on friendship, for example – and which amounted to a complete world view. Much has been written about the famous – or notorious – 'Bloomsbury voice', invented by Lytton Strachey and imitated by his acolytes, and described by Frances Partridge: "It had a life of its own, starting low and soft, rising to a faint scream, stopping altogether, swallowing itself, and then sinking to the depths again."[12] Thanks to the British Library's *Spoken Word* series of recordings we can listen to the analogues or variants of this voice, if not the genuine article, the *ur*-Strachean sound, on two CDs[13] from the BBC and British Library sound archives. They seem like voices from another world, impossibly plummy and patrician, perhaps because they *were* plummy and patrician, and because they learned to speak a century ago when, in the educated upper-middle class professional worlds they came from, it was perfectly natural to speak like that. The Woolfs themselves always insisted, quite rightly, that they were not at the very top of English society, merely middle (I would say upper-middle) class, but the middle classes had servants and lived in some comfort and were separated by an immense gulf from the working classes whose presence in their works is vestigial, though their old cooks and nannies loved them.

In this context there is the Joyce Problem. In a notorious diary entry for 16th August 1922, Virginia Woolf dismissed Joyce's *Ulysses*, as the "illiterate, underbred book... of a self taught working man." She later revealed a more nuanced understanding of Joyce and shouldn't be judged wholly on this outburst (she said later that she meant it was 'underbred' in a literary rather than a class sense) but the fact that she could use such terms offers an insight into the social values that had been implanted in her, that would become instinctive and natural.

Virginia Woolf's elder sister Vanessa, the artist who married Clive Bell, was, as were both Leonard and Virginia Woolf, very precise about the terminal dates and locations of this putatively non-existent

group. In her 1951 'Notes on Bloomsbury' (not published until 1997) Vanessa Bell explains how the Stephen sisters, Vanessa and Virginia, moved from their 'melancholy' home in Hyde Park Gate after the death of their rather demanding father, Sir Leslie Stephen, in 1904, to No 46 Gordon Square, Bloomsbury. "We knew no one living in Bloomsbury then and that I think was one of its attractions," she noted. It was convenient for her to have the Slade around the corner in Gower Street and she attended briefly as an art student. It all seemed to the Stephens girls like a new beginning and Vanessa Bell understandably dates the start of 'Bloomsbury' at 1904, where Leonard Woolf chose 1911 as the starting point. The outbreak of the First World War in 1914 is generally seen as the end of the original Bloomsbury phase but, of course, its members continued to paint, write, and think, long afterwards. No 46 Gordon Square was a rather cold house in 1904, heated by coal fires in old-fashioned open fireplaces "but it was exhilarating to have left the house [in Hyde Park Gate] in which had been so much gloom and depression, to have come to these white walls, large windows opening on to trees and lawns, to have one's own rooms, be master of one's own time, have all the things in fact which come as a matter of course to many of the young today but so seldom then, to young women at least."[14] Harold Nicholson noted: "It was a cold, grim house in a cold, grim district,"[15] and all Virginia's friends insisted that Bloomsbury was such an awful place that simply no one, my dear, would think of coming to visit them.

According to Vanessa Bell, they had not long been settled in to Gordon Square before her brother, Thoby, recently down from Cambridge and now reading for the Bar, started to draw together some of his university friends who were also trying to get launched in London. Thoby decided on a weekly 'at home' at No 46 and thus the famous 'Thursdays' began. The refreshments were mostly cocoa and biscuits, with an occasional whisky, but the real stimulant was that intoxicating Bloomsbury substance: talk. The nucleus of the

Bloomsbury group was Lytton Strachey, Clive Bell, Charles Tennyson, Hilton Young, Desmond McCarthy, Theodore Llewelyn Davies, Robin Mayor, many of whose names are forgotten now. Some, like Saxon Sydney Turner, who worked as a civil servant and walked across from his rooms in Great Ormond Street, are often mentioned in Bloomsbury reminiscences but have left little trace on the literary and intellectual landscape. Perhaps the most significant boldness was that two young women, Vanessa and Virginia, were allowed to enter what would normally have been, in the year 1905, an exclusively male company – and it was a company with no elders present. "What *did* we talk about?" Vanessa later asked herself. "The only true answer can be anything that came into our heads." There were no limits to what could be talked about and it did not always have to be serious for Thursdays sometimes included Adrian Stephen's dog, Hans, performing his trick of blowing out matches. The most important member of the Thursday evening group was, without doubt, Lytton Strachey, and his iconoclastic wit encouraged everyone else. "But only those first getting to know him well in the days when complete freedom of mind and expression were almost unknown, at least among men and women together, can understand what an exciting world of exploration of thought and feeling he seemed to reveal," wrote Vanessa Bell. "Perhaps it made a difference that no one... had any feelings to be considered. None of us had the slightest respect, for instance, for religion or religious questions." Strachey, son of a distinguished General, whose mother held society balls at their grand house at Lancaster Gate, was the perfect embodiment of this deliberate upper-middle class rebelliousness, that was relishing the intellectual freedoms of a new century and a modern movement in the arts climaxing in London in 1910 in the Post Impressionist Exhibition.

The sudden death of Thoby from typhoid in 1906 was a blow to this company and when Vanessa married Clive Bell in the spring of 1907, turfing out Virginia and Adrian from No 46, they went to Fitzroy Square where the Thursdays started up again, hosted by Virginia, who always insisted that Fitzroy Square was part of Bloomsbury. In a sense she was right because the sacred flame of Bloomsbury was rekindled there. She stayed in Fitzrovia until 1911 when, with Adrian, she moved to Brunswick Square. When she married Leonard Woolf in 1912 and went to live in Richmond (though she would be drawn back later by the siren call of Bloomsbury) a certain phase, according to Vanessa, had ended.

Virginia Woolf, in her posthumously published memoirs, *Moments of Being*, wrote of what she called 'Old Bloomsbury', the original circle that revolved around the hub of Thursdays in Gordon Square, and she shares her sister's view that the glory days were from 1904 to 1914. Woolf's account of 'Old Bloomsbury', her term for this *Echt*-Bloomsbury group, was delivered in 1920 to a meeting of The Memoir Club, a select group of around thirteen people, all of whom can safely be judged to be 'Bloomsberries', who met to read papers to each other in which, in true Bloomsbury fashion, nothing was held back (or that is what they believed). "46 Gordon Square," she wrote, "could never have meant what it did had not 22 Hyde Park Gate preceded it."[16] What she meant was that the house they had left behind, dominated by the moody, emotionally demanding, and controlling patriarch, Sir Leslie Stephen, made No 46 Gordon Square seem a liberation, a discovery of relative light and space that perfectly paralleled the Bloomsbury project of blowing away the fusty cobwebs of English Victorian and Edwardian convention, stuffiness, gloom, and restraint. Gordon Square was a new beginning. "When one sees it today [1920]," she admitted, "Gordon Square is not one of the most romantic of the Bloomsbury squares. It has neither the distinction of Fitzroy Square nor the majesty of Mecklenburgh Square. It is prosperous middle class and thoroughly mid-Victorian. But I can assure you that in October 1904 it was the most beautiful, the most exciting, the most romantic place in the world." She was overcome by the view from the first-floor drawing room window of abundant trees in leaf (it is no different today) glistening after rain "like the body of a seal". Even the Victorian portraits by G.F. Watts, the Dutch furniture, the blue china, which had cowered in the gloom of Hyde Park Gate "shone out for the first time in the drawing room at Gordon Square". It is true that various 'odd characters' from Bloomsbury's cast of eccentrics and loafers and members of the lower orders slunk past but they would not have got beyond the servants at the door. Most importantly of all there was space. She and Vanessa each had their own sitting room and the interior decoration swept away Victorian clutter and heavy William Morris wallpapers to replace them with plain distemper washes and consciously modern design ideas. All the fussy, dark domestic rituals of Hyde Park Gate were swept away too: "Everything was going to be new; everything was going to be different. Everything was on trial."

Life in this Bloomsbury honeymoon period was bliss; lunching, dining out, browsing in bookshops, going to concerts and picture-galleries, the Zoo, *Peter Pan*, and meeting dozens of artistic and socially well-connected people, breaking off occasionally to deliver an improving lecture on the Greek myths to working men at Morley College south of the Thames. But it was the 'at homes' that counted: "These Thursday evening parties were, as far as I am concerned, the germ from which sprang all that has since come to be called – in newspapers, novels, in Germany, in France – even, I daresay, in Turkey and Timbuktu – by the name of Bloomsbury." Woolf wanted to record these evenings but, as she admitted, talk (which was the essence of it) is "as elusive as smoke". Her brother Thoby, dubbed 'The Goth' by Lytton Strachey, had been the catalyst and he had a fondness for extravagant hype about the friends to whom he was just about to introduce his sisters which excited them. Some, like Strachey, needed no hype because the reality of this 'prodigious wit' outdid any advance publicity. They would talk about beauty and truth, and endless large abstractions, inspired by the Cambridge philosopher G.E. Moore, the intellectual godfather of Bloomsbury, whose *Principia Ethica*, published the year before the Stephens girls moved into No 46, was the secular bible of the group. It was especially exciting for them to be in a room talking about serious subjects with young men who would normally have had to present themselves to their mother and go through a series of polite social rituals before being allowed to speak to a member of the opposite sex. "The young men... had no 'manners' in the Hyde Park Gate sense. They criticised our arguments as severely as their own. They never seemed to notice how we were dressed or if we were nice looking or not." Suddenly the girls were liberated from the tyranny of having to be complimented on their hairdos or outfits rather than on what they had to say in debate. The precious words they wanted to hear were: "I must say you made your point rather well." They didn't mind at all that these earnest young men, many from Cambridge where they had belonged to The Society ('The Cambridge Apostles') were not very snappily dressed, though this horrified Henry James who exclaimed to a friend: "How could Leslie's daughters have taken up with young men like that?" For Virginia, however, this absence of the normal marriageable qualities was what validated their seriousness and attracted her to them. But in 1907, Vanessa did fall for one of them, Clive Bell, and married him and "the first chapter of Old Bloomsbury came to an end".

One other feature of the Thursdays was that a great many of the young men were homosexual, or, as Bloomsbury always put it,

'buggers', a word used to me in her nineties by the late Sybille Bedford (herself gay) when I interviewed her in Chelsea in the summer of 2000 for my biography of Aldous Huxley. "The society of buggers," Woolf pointed out, "has many advantages – if you are a woman. It is simple, it is honest, it makes one feel... in some respects at one's ease." But she nonetheless missed something – and she realised what it was when she went, one evening, from the restraint (perhaps a necessary restraint in days before the law relating to such things was changed in the 1960s) of James Strachey's bachelor rooms at Cambridge to the glitter and vivacity of dinner at No 44 Bedford Square with Lady Ottoline Morrell. What Woolf called Chapter Two of Old Bloomsbury began when Vanessa and Clive dined with connubial aplomb, deploying pretty eighteenth century silver at Gordon Square to demonstrate how "Bloomsbury rapidly lost its monastic character". It became a little less bluestocking and a little more social and frivolous. "It was in these years, from 1909 or 1910 to 1914, that there came the great expansion and development of Bloomsbury, that life seemed fullest of interest and promise and expansion of all kinds," Vanessa Bell claimed.

Virginia Woolf chose a story of another bugger to illustrate this. It is probably the most famous Bloomsbury anecdote because it captures the insouciant frankness and freedom that the Bloomsberries demanded as of right in an Edwardian world that, for everyone else, was so much more hidebound. She was visiting her sister at No 46 one spring evening, noting how a large Augustus John painting filled one wall, the hopelessly old-fashioned Victorian portraits of her parents by Watts, having been banished into store, when Lytton Strachey walked into the drawing room, pointed at a stain on Vanessa's white dress and inquired coolly: "Semen?" Woolf's first reaction was to ask herself whether, even here, even in Gordon Square, one could really say such a thing. But everyone immediately burst out laughing. "With that one word all barriers of reticence and reserve went down. A flood of the sacred fluid seemed to overwhelm us, Sex permeated our conversation.... We discussed copulation with the same excitement and openness that we had discussed the nature of good." They marvelled at how reticent and reserved they had been for so long. Even as recently as 1909 she and Clive had blushed when she merely asked him, on an express train in France, if he could let her get past in order to go to the lavatory. The new freedom seems to have turned out to involve "listening with rapt interest to the love affairs of buggers" and pouring scorn on traditional views of marriage. "So now there was nothing that one could say, nothing that one could not do, at 46 Gordon Square. It was, I think, a great advance in civilisation." Good old Lytton.

Not everyone, of course, shared this new freedom and there was a certain amount of scandal when, in 1911, Virginia moved into a shared house with Adrian Stephen, Maynard Keynes, Duncan Grant and Leonard Woolf at No 38 Brunswick Square. Her stepbrother George Duckworth came up from Charles Street in respectable St James (seemingly having forgotten his sexual abuse of her in childhood) to plead with Virginia to reconsider. Vanessa's retort that if anything went wrong the Foundling Hospital was on their doorstep scarcely mollified his fear and subsequently there were allegations of casual sex (Maynard Keynes having sex on a Brunswick Square sofa with Vanessa for example) and wild parties and general depravity practised by these "heartless, immoral and cynical" young people.

Was that it? Is that what 'Bloomsbury' amounts to? Upper-class self-indulgence and sexual freedom and a laughing resolve to *épater le bourgeois*? It is not likely that the group – and, more importantly, the group's actual products, the books and the paintings – would have exercised such an influence, and captured attention, for more than a century if it had been nothing more than an opportunity for us to yield to an appalled fascination with the antics of a bunch of arrogant toffs. Leonard Woolf, who married Virginia in 1912 in St Pancras Town Hall during a summer thunderstorm, in his version of Bloomsbury tries to establish its intellectual pedigree. Although he clearly rooted it in the society of Cambridge at the start of the twentieth century, in the circle of 'Apostles' around G.E. Moore, he dated its beginnings from 1911, a good seven years later than Virginia and Vanessa assumed in their accounts, and claims that when he returned from Ceylon where he had been working as a colonial administrator, he dined on 3rd July 1911 at No 46 Gordon Square with the Bells and at this point: "Bloomsbury had not yet actually come into existence."[17] He lists thirteen[18] people who formed the original Old

Bloomsbury, all of whom have been mentioned above, and seems to imply that it was only when they started to take up physical residence in "those nostalgic London squares" of Bloomsbury in numbers after 1911 that the Group could be said to exist properly. Like everyone else he insists that they were just a group of friends with roots specifically in Cambridge. Setting aside the three women in the list, nine of the ten men had known each other at Cambridge and of the ten men only Clive Bell, Adrian Stephen and Duncan Grant were not Apostles. They were, as Leonard Woolf puts it, "permanently inoculated with Moore and Moorism", adding that: "The main things which Moore instilled deep into our minds and characters were his peculiar passion for truth, for clarity and common sense, and a passionate belief in certain values."

This is the essence of the Bloomsbury style: whether one was writing fiction or philosophy or economic theory one wrote in ordinary lucid English. One can hear this in those British Library recordings mentioned above. Forget the patrician timbre of the voices, the old-fashioned chiselled articulations of another era, the key feature of this way of speaking or writing or thinking was its "clarity and common sense", the quality that shines through, for example, Leonard Woolf's four volumes of autobiography, or Clive Bell's *Art* or Roger Fry's *Vision and Design*, as far removed as it is possible to be from the specialised dialect employed by recent academic theory in all these subjects. For Leonard Woolf, Moore had exercised a Socratic influence on all these young men by asking the Greek philosopher's basic 'cathartic' question: "What do you mean by that?" It was, for him, a kind of intellectual purification: "Artistically the purification can, I think, be traced in the clarity, light, absence of humbug in Virginia's literary style and perhaps in Vanessa's painting. They have the quality noted by Maynard in Moorism, the getting rid of irrelevant extraneous matter." Cambridge and Moore had given the founders of Bloomsbury a shared intellectual foundation, a colour or temperament: "But we had no common theory, system, or principles which we wanted to convert the world to; we were not proselytizers, missionaries, crusaders, or even propagandists."

The significant phase of Bloomsbury ended with the First World War which not only marked the violent end of that phase of European civilization that had nourished the group's members but it found them marginalized in some sense. Weeding vegetables at Garsington, rather than dying in the trenches, many seemed bewildered by the war, coming at a time when their intellectual revolution should have delivered a post-Victorian brave new world of enlightened values, not the carnage of the Somme. There was something profoundly *inadequate* about Vanessa Bell's summing up in the 1950s: "Bloomsbury was not destroyed as probably many other circles were destroyed by the departure of all its young men to the wars. Perhaps one reason for much of the later abuse was that many were Conscientious Objectors. For some time they were let alone and quietly pursued their usual professions. Women of course were not conscripted during that war and could do as they liked. So for a time Bloomsbury still existed even if crushed and bored by the outer world. The excitement and joy had gone. The hostility of the general public was real now, no longer a ridiculous and even stimulating joke, and the dreariness of universal khaki seemed only too appropriate."[19]

It seemed, to Vanessa, as if the war were merely a rather irksome piece of bad taste.

BLOOMSBURY: THE END

I am back where I began, when this book first started to form in my mind, sitting on a bench in Russell Square on a freakishly hot day in the middle of May, with local kids jumping, screaming, shivering with cold and over-excitement as they dart in and out of the jets of water shooting up from the stone flags in the central space of the park. Tourists, dons, local mums, students, the usual Bloomsbury characters, come and go. And in my head a stray line from Philip Larkin's poem 'I Remember, I Remember' keeps buzzing at me: "Nothing, like something, happens anywhere." That isn't how it is meant to be. This is not 'anywhere' but one of the most famous of London's districts – for all the reasons I have been writing about. I have explored its history, topography, architecture, its contemporary face. I have talked to students, lawyers, shopkeepers, academics, booksellers and countless others. I have shared many memories of my own involvement with Bloomsbury over nearly forty years, as student, tourist, employee, resident, yet its essence remains tantalisingly elusive, and fresh, which is something of a relief. There is always something left to explore, to uncover, to realise for the first time. There is never any question of its losing its interest and appeal.

I look down at the book I have brought to read, escaping the late afternoon heat in the flat like so many others in the heart of the city on this sweltering day: *The London Adventure or The Art of Wandering*

(1924) by the Welsh writer Arthur Machen, a book I snapped up for the title alone when I came upon it in a Radnorshire bookseller's bargain back-room. It's an odd, digressive, book that has the feel of someone riffling through his bottom drawer and recycling whatever bits and pieces he chances to fish out. Machen is writing about the early years of the twentieth century, and his wanderings were through the newly developing streets of London north and east, as he puts it, of Gray's Inn Road and therefore just across my self-imposed boundary: "I found myself traversing unknown and unconjectured regions, happy as always in finding infinity around the corner in any street, within five minutes of anywhere." It is the same sense he had, as a boy, climbing up from his birthplace, Caerlon-on-Usk in Monmouthshire, to explore the magnificent loneliness of Mynydd Fawr. Mystery, the presence of other worlds and other consciousnesses, in close proximity to our own, is what Machen sought to convey in his stories. And the skilled urban wanderer can find this, perhaps, simply by turning the next corner, with ears and eyes open.

But this, I tell myself, is Bloomsbury, where universities, literary salons, reforming institutions gather in the common pursuit of enlightened values, dedicated to shining light rather than conjuring up the darkness of mystery. This central space of the articulate city exists under a bright spotlight and it is hard to find unexplored corners. Machen wrote of trying "to give the sense and feelings of lives that are lived there, remote from all thoughts of London, from all its central and mastering aims and visions and ambitions. Here live, I know, the people who are a little aside from all our tracks, and, perhaps, some of them have wisdom of their own or a folly of their own which differ from all our common systems of sapience or stultification."

Today a newsletter from the Green Party drops through my letterbox at Strachey Mansions. In it the writer Beatrix Campbell, who sought my vote recently as a local Green councillor in Bloomsbury Ward, writes that the residents of Bloomsbury in the summer of 2010 "feel under pressure – from high costs, growing inequality, traffic, pollution and a chronic shortage of affordable, energy-efficient housing". Are things that bad? Is the city a dysfunctional nightmare, a threat to the survival of the planet, a place of universal stress and *angst*? Or is it, what it has always been for me, a place of opportunity, not in the Dick Whittington sense of finding the streets paved with gold, but of discovery, of imaginative release, of stimulus.

Bloomsbury hasn't exhausted me yet. There is so much more exploring to be done, so much more to come.

Notes

1. Nicholas Murray, 'Carpetbagging in Bermondsey', *The London Review of Books*, 19 August, 1982
2. Miranda Seymour, *Ottoline Morrell: life on the grand scale* (1998), p397
3. Henry B Wheatley *London Past and Present* (1891) [revision of Peter Cunningham's 1849 *Handbook of London*] p134
4. Cited by E Beresford Chancellor, *London's Old Latin Quarter* (1930), p248
5. Cited by Negley Harte and John North, *The World of UCL 1828-1990* (1991), p10; see also David Taylor, *The Godless Students of Gower Street* (1968)
6. Kenneth Allott (ed), *Selected Poems of Winthrop Mackworth Praed* (1953), p276-7
7. Hermione Hobhouse, *Lost London* (1976) p84-5
8. Alan Crawford, *Oxford Dictionary of National Biography* entry
9. Cited by E Beresford Chancellor in *The History of the Squares of London Topographical and Historical* (1907) p243
10. Regina Marler, *Bloomsbury Pie: The Story of the Bloomsbury Revival* (1997) p282
11. Leonard Woolf, *Beginning Again: An Autobiography of the Years 1911 to 1918* (1964), p21
12. Cited by Marler, op. cit., p69
13. *The Bloomsbury Group* (2009), The British Library, NSACD-58-59.
14. Vanessa Bell, *Sketches in Pen and Ink* (1997), p
15. Harold Nicholson, *The Bloomsbury Group* (2009), The British Library, NSACD-58-59.
16. Virginia Woolf, 'Old Bloomsbury', *Moments of Being* (1976), p160
17. Leonard Woolf, op. cit., p22
18. Vanessa Bell, Clive Bell, Virginia Woolf, Leonard Woolf, Adrian Stephen, Lytton Strachey, Maynard Keynes, Duncan Grant, E.M. Forster, Saxon Sydney-Turner, Roger Fry, Desmond McCarthy, Molly McCarthy
19. Vanessa Bell, op. cit., p112

SQUARES	*STREETS*	*PLACES*
A Gordon Square	H Malet Street	O Brunswick Centre
B Tavistock Square	I Great Russell Street	P Foundling Museum
C Woburn Square	J Woburn Place	Q Charles Dickens Museum
D Torrington Square	K Cartwright Gardens	
E Brunswick Square	L Judd Street	
F Queen Square	M Great Ormond Street	
G Bloomsbury Square	N Lambs Conduit Street	

BIBLIOGRAPHY

Ackroyd, Peter. *London The Biography.* Vintage, 2001.
Anon. *Handbook to London As It Is.* John Murray, 1879.
Anon. *The Ambulator; or pocket companion for the tour of London and its envrirons.* 11th. Whittingham and Rowland, 1811.
Anon. *The Picture of London,* for 1815. 16th. Longman, 1815.
Barnes, William. *A Century of Camden Housing.* London Borough of Camden, 1971.
Bell, Quentin. *Bloomsbury.* Weidenfeld & Nicholson, 1968.
Bell, Vanessa. *Sketches in Pen and Ink.* Hogarth Press, 1997.
Bowers, Faith. *A Bold Experiment: The Story of Bloomsbury Chapel and Bloomsbury Central Baptist Church 1848-1999.* Bloomsbury Central Baptist Church, 1999.
Bradshaw, Tony. *A Bloomsbury Canvas: Reflections on the Bloomsbury Group.* Lund Humphries, 2001.
Bradshaw, Tony. *The Bloomsbury Artists: Prints and Book Design.* Scolar Press, 1999.
Brooker, Peter. *Bohemia in London: The Social Scene of Early Modernism.* Basingstoke: Palgrave Macmillan, 2007.
Brown, Walter E. *St Pancras Open Spaces and Disused Burial Grounds.* St Pancras Borough Council, 1911.
Brown, Walter E. *The Records of St Pancras.* St Pancras Borough Council, 1905.
Brown, Walter E. *The St Pancras Book of Dates.* St Pancras Borough Council, 1908.
Campbell, Roy. *The Georgiad: a satirical fantasy in verse.* Boriswood, 1931.
Chancellor, E Beresford. *London's Old Latin Quarter: being an account of Tottenham Court Road and its immediate suuroundings.* Jonathan Cape, 1930.
Chancellor, E Beresford. *The History of The Squares of London Topgraphical and Historical.* Kegan Paul, Trench, Trübner & Co, 1907.
Cherry, Bridget, and Nikolaus Pevsner. *The Buildings of England, London 4: North.* Penguin, 1998.
Clinch, George. *Bloomsbury and St Giles's Past and Present: with historical and antiquarian notices of the vicinity.* Truslove and Shirley, 1890.
Davis, Eliza Jeffries. *The University Site, Bloomsbury.* London Topographical Record, 1936.
De la Ruffinière du Prey, Pierre. *Hawksmoor's London Churches: architecture and theology.* Chicago: University of Chicago, 2000.
Dickens, Charles. *Sketches by Boz.* 1839.
Diski, Jenny. *Skating to Antarctica.* Granta, 1997.
Dobie, Rowland. *The History of the United Parishes of St Giles in the Fields and St George, Bloomsbury.* 2nd. Rowland Dobie, 1834.
Downes, Kerry. *Hawksmoor.* Thames and Hudson, 1969.
Empson, William. *Selected Letters of William Empson.* John Haffenden. Oxford: Oxford University Press, 2006.
English, Isobel. *Every Eye.* Persephone Books, 2000.

Fargue, Léon-Paul. *Le Piéton de Paris*. Gallimard, 1939.
Gatt-Rutter, John, and Brian Moloney (eds). *This England is So Different: Italo Svevo's London Writings*. Troubador, 2003.
Gatt-Rutter, John. *Italo Svevo: A Double Life*. Oxford University Press, 1988.
Grant, Joy. *Harold Monro and the Poetry Bookshop*. 1967.
Grosch, Alfred. *St Pancras Pavements*. John Gifford, 1947.
Haffenden, John. *William Empson: Among the Mandarins*. Oxford: Oxford University Press, 2005.
Harrison, J F C. *A History of the Working Men's College 1854-1954*. Routledge & Kegan Paul, 1954.
Hart, Vaughan. *Nicholas Hawksmoor: rebuilding ancient wonders*. New Haven: Yale University Press, 2002.
Harte, Negley, and John North. *The World of UCL: 1828-1990*. UCL, 1991.
Henderson, John N. *A History of the Museum Tavern in Bloomsbury*. Blemund's Books, 1989.
Henrey, Mrs Robert. *Bloomsbury Fair*. J.M. Dent, 1955.
Hobhouse, Hermione. *Lost London: a century of demolition and decay*. Macmillan, 1976.
Hobhouse, Hermione. *Thomas Cubitt: Master Builder*. Management Books 2000, 1995.
Holroyd, Michael. *Lytton Strachey*. Chatto & Windus, 1994.
Holroyd, Michael. *Lytton Strachey and the Bloomsbury Group: His Work, Their Influence*. Penguin, 1971.
Hughes, Ted. *Birthday Letters*. Faber and Faber, 1998.
James, Henry. *Collected Travel Writings*. New York: Library of America, 1993.
Larkin, Philip. *Collected Poems*. Faber, 1988.
Lee, Hermione. *Virginia Woolf*. Chatto & Windus, 1996.
Lehmann, John. Holborn. Macmillan, 1970.
MacNeice, Louis. *The Collected Poems of Louis MacNeice* (1979)
Maitland, William. *The History of London from Its Foundation to the Present Time*. London, 1769.
Marler, Regina. *Bloomsbury Pie: The Story of the Bloomsbury Revival*. Virago, 1997.
Melhuish, Clare. *The Life and Times of the Brunswick, Bloomsbury*. Camden History Society, 2006.
Miles, Barry. *In The Sixties*. Jonathan Cape, 2002.
Murray, Nicholas. *Aldous Huxley: An English Intellectual*. Little, Brown, 2002.
Murray, Nicholas. *Remembering Carmen*. Seren, 2003.
Murray, Nicholas. *World Enough and Time: The Life of Andrew Marvell*. Little, Brown, 1999.
Noorthouck, John. *A New History of London*. R Baldwin, 1773.
Palmer, Samuel. *St Pancras*. Samuel Palmer, 1870.
Parton, John. *Some Account of the Hospital and Parish of St Giles in the Fields, Middlesex*. Luke Hansard, 1822.

Pearce, Joseph. *Bloomsbury and Beyond: The Friends and Enemies of Roy Campbell.* Harper Collins, 2001.
Pugh, Gillian. *London's Forgotten Children: Thomas Coram and the Foundling Hospital.* Stroud: Tempus, 2007.
Pritchett, V.S. *London Perceived.* The Hogarth Press, 1986.
Reed, Christopher. *Bloomsbury Rooms: Modernism, Subculture, and Domesticity.* New Haven: Yale University Press, 2004.
Reid, Christopher. *The Song of Lunch* (2009)
Society, Camden History. *Streets East of Bloomsbury.* Camden History Society, 2008.
Society, Camden History. *Streets of Bloomsbury and Fitzrovia.* Camden History Society, 1997.
Strype, John. *A Survey of the Cities of London and Westminster by John Stow.* 6th. London, 1854.
Summerson, John. *Georgian London.* Pleiades Books, 1945.
Tames, Richard. *Bloomsbury Past: a visual history.* Historical Publications, 1993.
Taylor, David. *The Godless Students of Gower Street.* University College London Union, 1968.
Thomas, Philip. *Auguste Comte and Richard Congreve: Discourse Given at the Church of Humanity, Chapel Street, Holborb, July 3, 1910.* Watts & Co, 1910.
Thomas, Philip. *Our Church and Faith of Humanity: An Opening Discourse Delivered at the Church of Humanity, Chapel Street, Holborn on the 9th Day of the Month of Moses in the year 56 of the Positivist Era (Being the 9th January, 1910 of the Christian Era)* (1910). Watts & Co, 1910.
Thomson, Gladys Scott. *The Russells in Bloomsbury 1669-1771.* Jonathan Cape, 1940.
Tindall, Gillian. *Footprints in Paris.* 2009.
Tindall, Gillian. *The Fields Beneath.* Maurice Temple Smith, 1977.
Wheatley, Henry B. *London Past and Present: its history, associations, and traditions.* John Murray, 1891.
Willis, J.H. *Leonard and Virginia Woolf as Publishers: The Hogarth Press, 1917-41.* Charlottesville: University Press of Virginia, 1992.
Wilson, Jean Moorcroft. *Virgina Woolf's London: a guide to Bloomsbury and beyond.* Tauris Parke, 2000.
Woolf, Leonard. *An Autobiography: 1, 1880-1911.* Oxford University Press, 1990.
Woolf, Leonard. *An Autobiography: 2, 1911-1969.* Oxford University Press, 1990.
Woolf, Virginia. *Moments of Being.* Jeanne Schulkind. Harcourt Brace, 1976.

THE PHOTOGRAPHS

THE AUTHOR

Nicholas Murray was born in Liverpool, and lives in Wales and London. He is a widely acclaimed biogapher having written the first life of Bruce Chatwin, followed by works on Matthew Arnold, Andrew Marvell, Aldous Huxley (shortlisted for the Marsh Biography Prize) and Franz Kafka. He is also the author of two novels, *A Short Book About Love* and *Remembering Carmen*, and his poetry and other various work has appeared in the *Times Literary Supplement, Independent, Tribune, Guardian, Jewish Chronicle, New Welsh Poetry Review, Planet* and *Oxford Poetry*.

INDEX